WITH OUR PAST

ESSAYS ON THE HISTORY OF MISHAWAKA

PETER J. DE KEVER

With Our Past – Essays on the History of Mishawaka
ISBN 1-893270-17-3
Library of Congress Control Number: 2003105905

Printed in the USA by Evangel Press, Nappanee, Indiana.

For my parents, Joe and Mary Ann De Kever

CONTENTS

PART III

EVENTS

INTRODUCTION

❦

"How will we know it's us without our past?"

John Steinbeck asked this question in **The Grapes of Wrath**, expressing the concerns of Dust Bowl migrants forced to leave Oklahoma for an uncertain future in California.

Implicit in Steinbeck's question is a salient American conflict: How do we maintain healthy ties to the past while living in the present and preparing for the future? Closely related is the challenge of preserving the distinctiveness of local communities against the homogenizing forces of commercial mass culture and a mobile society. Contemporary writers such as William Least Heat-Moon and Scott Russell Sanders have reflected extensively on this issue.

Many American communities have discovered that the best way to celebrate their uniqueness is to preserve their history through museums, restoring historic buildings, naming streets and parks with an eye to the past, erecting statues with historical themes, and writing about subjects of local historic significance.

Mishawaka, too, has struggled to preserve its identity and history. Even in the 1930s, historian Vincent Brunner warned about South Bend, the "octopus to the West...trying to engulf and absorb Mishawaka" and the need for Mishawaka to remain "a distinct and separate community with its own inspiration." Brunner's concerns remain today as Mishawaka suffers from a large transient population, lack of respect for its historic buildings, a decline in locally-owned businesses, and civic leaders who have sold out the community and weakened Mishawaka's identity and autonomy. Of particular concern are today's Mishawakans under age 30, who feel less personal identification with Mishawaka as a distinct place than has any preceding generation in the city's history.

This book uses history to help preserve and enhance the sense of unique identity that Mishawakans have about their community. My hope also is that the subjects included here offer insight into the lives and achievements of interesting people, some still alive, but many who are long since deceased. These essays should encourage readers to look more closely at the places that comprise our community, to understand that historically significant events do happen here, and that people of greatness have left their mark on Mishawaka. History surrounds us.

Steinbeck worried about who we would be without our past. My intent here is to encourage readers to live **with** our past, to renew the connections we have to the history of Mishawaka.

With our past, we are reminded of who came before us and how our community developed.

With our past, we know ourselves.

With our past, we are inspired to be more than who we are.

This book is not a comprehensive, chronological survey of Mishawaka history. **Indiana's Princess City**, written by Janice Bridges in 1976, provides such a history that covers Mishawaka's first 100 years. Likewise, I have avoided topics featured in **A Mishawaka Mosaic**, edited by David Eisen for the sesquicentennial in 1983. Some subjects in Mishawaka history have been so frequently discussed in these books or featured in local newspapers that I do not feel I could contribute any new understanding about them. As a result, this book includes no essays on such topics as the Kamm and Schellinger Brewery, the Fire of 1872, the Beiger Mansion, or the Dodge Manufacturing Company. Worthy subjects like these have been addressed by writers whose work can readily be found on the shelves or in the files of the Mishawaka-Penn-Harris Public Library.

Instead, this book introduces readers to historical topics that either have never before been written about or that are not well known by the community. Rather than exhausting the subjects in Mishawaka history that merit writing about, this book is instead a sampling of some topics that have been of interest to me in my research and writing over the last several years.

I hope these essays inspire a greater interest in Mishawaka's history, prompting readers to take on the role of historian themselves, by writing about stories in their family history, researching the house they live in, or recording the memories of an aged relative or neighbor.

Most of these essays were first published in the **Mishawaka Enterprise** and the "Through the Years" or "Hometown" sections of the **South Bend Tribune**. Each essay, though, has been substantially revised, corrected, and expanded for this book. "Second Chances," "Year of the Kingsmen," and "They Finished Like Conquerors" have never before been published.

The essays are organized into people, places, and events, and then are presented chronologically within those sections. I struggled with classifying some essays, which do not always neatly fit into just one of these three categories. For example, the opening of the Tivoli Theater was a specific event, but the essay also profiles that significant place in 1925.

The essays about the cross country and academic teams are as much about the people who lived those experiences as they are about the culminating events of those seasons.

Just as fiction is driven by characterization, so is history the product of interaction among people, circumstances, and location.

My interests in writing about these subjects have varied origins. The research into the Powell family and the early history of African Americans in Mishawaka had its genesis in a conversation with David Eisen. He mentioned Elijah Powell as an interesting subject no one had written about, a comment I mentally filed away until I came across Powell's obituary while randomly looking through microfilm. While I was researching the origins of Normain Heights, I discovered articles about the 1948 and 1949 Mishawaka High School cross country state runner-up teams. Other subjects have come from recommendations by people in the community who recognized the historical value of the topic. For example, the oral history interview with Helen Doolittle was done at the suggestion of her grandson. The portrait of my grandfather results from years of hearing stories about him, while other topics, such as the Penn academic state championships, I have experienced personally.

Researching and writing about these topics has strengthened my own personal attachment to Mishawaka. While some of these writings focus more on places and events, they all include individuals whose lives are worthy of remembering. I have come to admire many of the people featured in these essays. It is a privilege to tell their stories.

Part I

PEOPLE

CHAPTER 1

FOUNDING FATHER: ALANSON HURD AND LIFE AFTER MISHAWAKA

Dodge, Beiger, and Eberhart are all names associated with the industrial development of Mishawaka in the late nineteenth century. Influential as these men were, none was one of Mishawaka's Founding Fathers, the generation that carved a town out of the wilderness along the banks of the St. Joseph River.

Foremost among those Mishawaka pioneers was the "Father of Mishawaka," Alanson Mead Hurd. In 1901 the book **South Bend and Mishawaka** proclaimed, "The city of Mishawaka owes its inception to Divine Providence and the genius, energy and progressive spirit of Alanson M. Hurd." A century later, though, Hurd is less known by Mishawakans than the later manufacturers for whom he blazed the trail.

Alanson Hurd was born near Ballston, New York, twenty miles north of Albany, on January 9, 1804. At age 22, Hurd made his way, probably via the Erie Canal, to Detroit, where he went into the iron business. His great-granddaughter, Bessie Celeste Hurd Forster, wrote that Hurd was "interested in Chemistry and Metallurgy...Great-grand-father joined a group of men going west to find a more durable iron ore to make into stoves that would not melt down with the use of hard

Alanson Hurd was born near Ballston, New York, on January 9, 1804. This photo was taken in Ballston in 2000.

Sarah Lefferts Hurd and Alanson Mead Hurd are shown here, c. 1870, after their move to Fort Atkinson, Wisconsin.

coal. They went to Detroit and great grandfather sent for great grandmother." In 1827 Hurd married Sarah Lefferts, a native of Mayfield, New York, near Ballston.

In 1832 Hurd noted reports of large bog iron deposits in the St. Joseph River Valley and hoped to construct a blast furnace in the area. A low-grade ore, bog iron can be melted and converted into pig iron, usable for manufacturing. Expecting the valley's settlements to grow, the entrepreneurial Hurd saw large profit potential in developing the area's iron resources. In June 1832 Hurd sent William Earl to scout out the best location to build an iron works. Earl found a large bog iron deposit at the "Twin Branches" 2 1/2 miles upriver from present-day downtown Mishawaka, as well as deposits elsewhere in the area.

Later that year, Hurd traveled to St. Joseph County to purchase ore and water rights to build a blast furnace in the Twin Branches. When Hurd saw the 2'9" fall of the rapids at the site of the present-day dam near Central Park, he was convinced that location's water power made it a better site for the iron works. Early Mishawaka historian George Merrifield noted in the **Mishawaka Enterprise** in 1859, "The foresight and sagacity of Mr. Hurd were eminently justified in the result."

On January 1, 1833, Hurd purchased school section 16 (today much of central Mishawaka) for $1.25 an acre. The first building erected in Hurd's settlement was a large frame structure that served first as workers' quarters and later as a general store for A.M. Hurd & Company. By winter the blast furnace was built (near where the police station stands today) along with other buildings needed for the iron operation.

While the iron works was under construction, Hurd also directed his attention to the development of the adjacent town. He sold most of the land he had bought to developers eager to invest in a growing village. The town of St. Joseph Iron Works was laid out in the summer of 1833. A year later, Henry Yerrington, Hurd's clerk and bookkeeper, suggested the town be named Mishawaka, when the government established a post office in the settlement.

Hurd sought settlers and workers, appealing to his contacts in Detroit and his family back East. He advertised in the **Michigan Statesman** and **St. Joseph Chronicle**:

Wanted—At the St. Joseph Iron Works, Indiana, a number of steady temperate laborers; to whom from fourteen to fifteen dollars per month will be given. Mishawaka, Indiana March 1834

The town grew quickly, and new settlers included Philo Hurd (Alanson's father), cousins Orlando and Elliot Hurd, and grandfather Mead Hurd. Mead, a Revolutionary War veteran, died a few weeks after arriving in the settlement and is buried in Mishawaka's City Cemetery, along with Elliot, Philo, and other family. In the summer of 1834, Alanson and Philo were among the first members of the new Presbyterian Church in Mishawaka. Alanson donated the lot for the church.

In 1834 the iron works began smelting iron ore into pig iron, and orders began coming in from as far north as the Grand River in Michigan and as far south as Indianapolis. Most of the iron was used for castings, such as stoves, kettles, plows, and gears for mills. The rest of the pig iron was shipped around the lakes back to Detroit or used by local blacksmiths.

Local historian Merle Blue has noted that from 1835-1845 "Mishawaka was the largest center of heavy industry, not just in St. Joseph County, but in the entire Great Lakes area west of Detroit." In fact, Mishawaka's iron manufacturing led Indiana Governor David Wallace to boast in 1838, "Mishawaka, South Bend, and their vicinity, bid fair to become ere long the Pittsburgh of Indiana."

Alanson Hurd was sole proprietor of the St. Joseph Iron Works until December 1834, when, perhaps needing more capital, he formed the St. Joseph Iron Company with three other partners. Hurd was its first president.

In the fall of 1835, Alanson Hurd lost in a court case involving William Earl, who said Hurd had hired him to scout for iron ore deposits near Ypsilanti, Michigan, with the hopes of building an iron works there. Earl alleged that their arrangement was that if adequate ore was found, Earl would be given a share in the iron works built there. If ore was insufficient and no iron works built, then Earl would be reasonably compensated for his services. Not enough ore was found to build the iron works, but Earl brought Hurd to court because Hurd had not paid him for his scouting. A St. Joseph County jury ordered Hurd to pay him $150 in damages.

Another case between Hurd and Earl dealt with payment for pork used to feed the iron workers. Hurd lost and incurred $258.28 in additional debt.

These and other expenses may have been large enough to force Hurd out of business, and in 1836 he retired from the iron works.

Sometime after 1840, the Father of Mishawaka left the town he created and moved to Waterloo, New York, for four years. The Hurds came back to Michigan and lived in Union City, Coldwater, and Sturgis Prairie until 1852, when they settled in Lake Mills, Wisconsin, fifty miles west of Milwaukee.

In the early 1850s, Lake Mills probably reminded Hurd of Mishawaka in the 1830s. **The Wisconsin Gazetteer** in 1853 reported that Lake Mills had a population of 400, with fifty homes, several stores, an iron foundry, and several other manufacturers. The young village might have appealed to Hurd's interest in promising settlements developing out of the frontier. Its proximity to the growing iron industry around Dodge County may also have attracted Hurd.

The Hurds lived in Lake Mills for a year and then moved to nearby Fort Atkinson, a bustling village of 750 straddling the Rock River. Featuring several blacksmith's shops and other small manufacturers, Fort Atkinson's bright future was assured when the railroad reached it in the 1850s. The village doubled its population between 1850 and 1860 as many others like Hurd saw the area's economic potential.

Hurd may have followed his son Henry to the Fort Atkinson area. In 1853 Henry Hurd opened a store in Fort Atkinson that specialized in stoves, iron products, machinery for mills, tinware, and stove pipes. Perhaps the expertise Alanson developed in the iron industry in Detroit and Mishawaka was passed along to his son in this business venture.

The 1860 Fort Atkinson town directory listed Alanson Hurd as a "retired merchant," but in April 1861 President Lincoln named him the town's postmaster, a job he held until January 1865. Postmasters of that era achieved their position largely through political connections, which suggests Hurd had acquired a good measure of influence and regard in his new hometown.

Hurd also was an active member of the Congregational Society in Fort Atkinson and helped construct the Society's first church building in the village.

Alanson Hurd lived out the rest of his life in Fort Atkinson and died there on October 6, 1877. In his obituary, the **Jefferson County Union** eulogized Hurd as "one of our best known and most respected citizens...a man of more than usual intelligence and ability...accurate and honest in his dealings with men, and in dying has left 'what is more to be desired than great riches'-- a good name."

He and his wife of fifty years-- who died in 1888-- are buried in Fort Atkinson's Evergreen Cemetery.

Alanson Hurd and his wife are buried in Evergreen Cemetery, Fort Atkinson, Wisconsin.

Alanson Hurd transformed wilderness into a manufacturing center, but the mill town on the St. Joseph River eventually grew far beyond the vision of its founder. Although no statues, parks, or schools have yet been named for Hurd, his monument is a growing, vibrant city that thousands call home. Their stories over the last 170 years are the legacy of the Father of Mishawaka.

CHAPTER 2

"THE VETERAN BARBER" ELIJAH HASTINGS POWELL AND THE EARLY AFRICAN AMERICAN COMMUNITY OF MISHAWAKA

Efforts to document and honor Mishawaka's diverse ethnic heritage have frequently centered around the immigration of Belgians and Italians, and, before them, Germans and Irish. In 1993 these immigrants' contributions to the Princess City were memorialized with a beautiful sculpture near the intersection of Main and Front streets in downtown Mishawaka.

Historians, though, have left virtually unstudied the origins and development of Mishawaka's small African American population. African Americans today comprise 4.3% of Mishawaka's 46,000 citizens, or roughly 2000 people. This segment of Mishawaka and its interaction with the white majority merit exploration in greater detail.

Such an extensive study exceeds the scope of this essay, which examines the beginnings of Mishawaka's African American population, focusing on one man and his family, who were at the center of the

Mishawaka African American community for nearly forty years. Elijah Hastings Powell came to Mishawaka as a barber in 1868 and lived here until until his death in 1906. Powell's story offers insight into the lives of African Americans in Indiana and Mishawaka during the nineteenth and early twentieth centuries.

Roots in Owen County

Elijah Powell was born October 2, 1841, near Spencer, Indiana, in rural Owen County, northwest of Bloomington.

Elijah's father, Farrow, was born in North Carolina in 1809. Farrow's mother was white and African American, and his father, Eliga, was Native American. Farrow married Elizabeth Walden in 1829. They had two children born in North Carolina and migrated north in 1833, traveling 60 days by ox cart to Terre Haute, where they stayed for a year. The Powells then settled near Spencer in 1834, where five more

Marie Johnson Moore painted this portrait of her grandfather, Elijah Powell.

children were born. Elizabeth died in 1841 due to complications from the birth of Elijah and his twin sister. Farrow remarried in 1844 to Rebecca Maria Bass, who, in 1837, at age 13, also had come from North Carolina to Indiana. Rebecca and Farrow had nine children together.

Emma Lou Thornbrough's **The Negro in Indiana before 1900** and **Indiana's African American Heritage**, edited by Wilma Gibbs, offer much background on Elijah Powell's historical era.

The migration of both whites and free African Americans from North Carolina to Indiana was already an established pattern by the 1830s. An 1830 North Carolina law required manumitted slaves to leave the state within 90 days. Quakers often acted as trustees for these freed slaves, helping ensure their safe transport to the free states. Some of these freed slaves went to Liberia, but most ended up in the Old Northwest, where laws allowed their resettlement.

Most of the African American settlers coming into Indiana before the Civil War were from the upper South. The largest single group, like the Powells, came from North Carolina (1,426), according to the 1850 census, the first to list birthplace. North Carolina, along with Virginia and Maryland, had the largest populations of free African Americans, some of whom, like Farrow's family, had never been slaves.

Many African Americans settled together when they reached Indiana, and more than twenty settlement communities have been identified in Indiana. As a result of this migration, Indiana's African American population grew from 1,420 in 1820, to 7,168 in 1840, to 11,262 in 1850.

When the Powells came to Indiana in the 1830s, they would have been met with conflicting attitudes and policies. The white majority in Indiana often saw African Americans as poor, uneducated aliens whose settlement was undesired. They were denied voting rights and an equal education. African Americans also had difficulty getting into skilled trades; as a result, few entered the middle class and most lived in rural poverty.

Despite these obstacles, Indiana was still attractive to African American settlers from the South. In fact, Owen County historian

Elijah Hastings Powell was born on October 2, 1841, on this farm west of Spencer, Indiana.

Roger Peterson suggests there was a relatively high degree of acceptance and integration of African Americans in that county. County records, he notes, do not distinguish much between whites and African Americans, and African Americans were substantial property owners, bought and sold land with whites, and were able to use the courts.

In 1839 Farrow Powell bought his first land a mile west of Spencer in Owen County's Washington Township. He purchased 37 acres and then a few days later 40 acres of adjoining government land. It is probably on that farm, just west of today's Owen Valley High School, where Elijah Powell was born and spent his early childhood.

Living off the land was typical for African Americans in antebellum Indiana. Most made their living through farming, although Powell was in the minority who owned the land they worked. In 1850, 976 of the 2,150 African Americans in the state were farmers, and another 720 were laborers, usually on farms.

By March 1847, as their family grew, Farrow and Rebecca purchased

160 acres in Marion Township, ten miles west of Spencer. Farrow acquired this land from the United States government, and purchased 40 adjoining acres from the Wabash and Erie Canal in 1849 and 40 more acres from Rebecca's step-father, Benjamin Bass, in 1850.

By the 1850 census, the Powells and their African American settlement had grown considerably from a decade before. There were nine children, and Elijah's twin sister had died. Farrow's brother Eaton and his wife and one-year-old daughter were living on Farrow's farm, probably as tenants or laborers. By this time, a relatively sizable community of African Americans had developed in Marion Township. African American migration into the township had been underway since the mid-1830s with purchases of land from the government. By the mid-1850s, this community grew to 100-150 people, and African Americans owned almost all the land in sections 27 and 28 of Marion Township. Farrow Powell's farm was in section 28.

This township was a good settlement site. In addition to the agricultural productivity, the area was endowed with hardwood forests and accessible coal deposits as a cheap fuel supply. Nineteenth century historians described Marion Township as possessing "nutritious qualities" in "the native grasses" that made raising livestock successful.

An 1850 agricultural census reveals much about the Powells' farm, where Elijah spent his later childhood. They had 240 acres, valued at $1000, which tied the Powells for having the most land wealth of any African Americans in the township. Farrow's farm equipment was worth $50, and he had two horses, seven head of cattle, 25 sheep, and 20 pigs. Altogether, his livestock was valued at $140. Powell's main crop was corn, with 300 bushels produced during the previous year, along with oats, wool, and a small quantity of potatoes. Butter and flax also were products of the Powell farm. These crops, in varying proportions, were typical of the other farms in Marion Township.

By the early 1850s, the climate for African Americans had begun to change for the worse in Indiana and Owen County. Migration into the state stagnated, and Indiana fell victim to the conservatism that afflicted much of the North. As the South became more sensitive to Northern anti-slavery rhetoric and actions, states like Indiana tried not to provoke their Southern neighbors by encouraging African American rights and settlement. The Fugitive Slave Law of 1850 also lowered migration and contributed to a more hostile environment for African Americans. Indiana's 1851 constitution placed further restrictions on African Americans, and official state policy for a while was to finance resettlement in Liberia.

The Owen County African American settlement began a rapid decline during the 1850s and was gone shortly after the Civil War. In 1848 Farrow sold his 77 acres near Spencer, and in 1852 he sold his 236-acre farm in Marion Township for $1800. The Powells then may have moved near Terre Haute for several years before migrating to northern Indiana.

Moving to South Bend

The Powells came to St. Joseph County in 1857. Farrow believed he could do better financially in the northern part of the state, and moved his family to a farm two miles south of South Bend. They stayed there two years until moving to 428 South Main Street in downtown South Bend. Farrow made land investments in South Bend and the surrounding countryside, including purchasing 120 acres in the Huggart African American settlement ten miles south of South Bend. Farrow Powell was one of the wealthiest of the 88 African Americans in the county in 1860.

Elijah in the Civil War

On November 23, 1863, Elijah Powell enlisted in the 1st Michigan Colored Infantry Regiment, which mustered into federal service in Detroit in February 1864. Elijah's decision to join the Union army was doubtless influenced by the enlistment of his brothers Colonel, Larkin, and James. Elijah and Larkin enlisted as "colored," while Colonel and James were light-skinned enough to "pass" in white regiments. In 1860 Colonel Powell, the first member of the Powell family to come to Mishawaka, had been a barber in downtown Mishawaka.

Early in the war, President Lincoln and other Northern leaders would not consider using African American troops, fearful of putting guns in the hands of what many saw as an inferior race. They also were sensitive about alienating the slaveholding border states like Kentucky and Maryland, which had stayed in the Union. Nonetheless, as the carnage dragged on and the Emancipation Proclamation was announced in September 1862, Lincoln permitted the War Department to form colored units. This provoked hysteria in Indiana, where some feared white soldiers would not volunteer if African Americans were in the army. Regardless, the federal Enrollment Act of March 1863 made all adult males, regardless of race, subject to the draft.

Some African Americans in Indiana would not wait for the state to open up its units to them and left to join the Massachusetts 54th Colored Infantry. This unit began recruiting in February 1863 and went to other states to get enough volunteers to form a full regiment, around a thousand men. Prior to the formation of Michigan colored regiments, men from that state also went to the Massachusetts colored regiments.

Even as late as August 1863, Governor Oliver P. Morton rejected the requests of African Americans in Indianapolis to arm themselves as part of the Indianapolis Home Guard.

Public opinion in Indiana began to change during 1863 as newspapers reported the valor of regiments like the 54th. In July, August, and September 1863, the 54th had participated in efforts to capture Battery Wagner, near Charleston Harbor. Their losses and exceptional performance in battle had begun to reshape whites' opinions of African American soldiers.

Maybe more influential on Hoosier public opinion was Indiana's difficulty in filling its quota of volunteers and the prospect of a draft. African American volunteers became a solution to the problem of drafting white soldiers. By November 1863 Morton exercised this option and encouraged the creation of colored regiments from Indiana.

This change of heart was too late for some Hoosiers, including Elijah Powell. In addition to the African Americans from Indiana who went into the Massachusetts regiments, others enlisted in the ranks of other states, including Michigan's First Colored Infantry.

By the end of the war, between 800 and 1,537 African Americans from Indiana served in the military. This was a fairly high percentage of the eligible age group. The Union Army had 186,017 African American soldiers, with most coming from slave states and only 33,000 from Northern free states.

Powell's service in a colored regiment came with dangers and inequities white soldiers did not have. The Confederate government had threatened to shoot or enslave any captured African American soldiers and any whites who commanded them. Also, despite early promises of equal pay and treatment, it was not until 1864 that Congress ordered that African American soldiers receive equal pay, equipment, and rations.

When Elijah Powell's 1st Michigan Colored Infantry Regiment left Detroit on March 28, 1864, headed for Annapolis, Maryland, its enrollment was 895 officers and men. Like all colored regiments, it was staffed with only white officers. Its ultimate destination was Hilton Head, South Carolina, a staging area for operations in the Charleston area and along the coast. Later, the War Department changed the 1st's designation to the 102nd Regiment of United States Colored Infantry.

The 102nd reached Hilton Head, twenty miles northwest of Savannah, on April 19, 1864, and guarded various points along the South Carolina coast, being based at Port Royal, near Hilton Head. In early August the regiment was sent to Jacksonville, Florida, and remained in the state for a month. Just once did it engage the enemy, when Confederate cavalry attacked and were quickly repulsed. Powell's regiment had several long marches in Florida but minimal combat.

The real fighting for the 102nd came after it returned to South Carolina and was put on picket and fatigue duty near Beaufort, just north of Port Royal. Three hundred men from the 102nd were part of a 5000-man force called the Coast Division, which had the task of aiding General Sherman's March to the Sea by cutting the Charleston and Savannah Railroad near Pocotaligo, twenty miles northwest of Beaufort. The detachment from the 102nd joined the 54th Massachusetts and other units in late November. They moved by fleet up the Broad River to Boyd's Landing. From there, action occurred at Honey Hill, where the Confederates had built earthen fortifications to help keep open the railroad. The 102nd was the last to reach Honey Hill on November 30, and a number of its officers and men were shot while hauling artillery. The Union lost the battle, which allowed the Confederates to remain in Savannah. The Union forces next invaded Devereaux Neck, trying to cut the railroad between the Coosawhatchie River and the Tullifinny River. On December 9 the 102nd was part of the main Union line that cannonaded the railroad. During these battles, 65 officers and men from the 102nd were killed or wounded.

In late January 1865, Powell's entire regiment was positioned at Pocotaligo and formed a brigade with the 54th Massachusetts and other regiments. On February 7 they skirmished with Georgia troops, and on February 8, four of the 102nd's companies engaged in light skirmishing and destroyed part of the railroad, blocking the Confederate path south. On February 14 the 102nd pursued a rebel force escaping north to Ashepoo. There, bridges had been burned, and the Union troops crossed the Ashepoo River in boats, driving off a small enemy force.

By February 19 Charleston was evacuated, and the 102nd entered the city later that month. The regiment moved to Savannah in March, part of a colored brigade occupying the city.

From there the 102nd and 54th were sent to Georgetown, South Carolina, a port town sixty miles north of Charleston. General Sherman had ordered troops inland to destroy Confederate railcars trapped by destroyed bridges. On April 7 the 102nd's left wing destroyed the Kingstree Bridge across the Black River west of Georgetown. There, they met a small Confederate force. On April 9 they moved toward Manchester and burned a covered railroad bridge, several rail cars, 200 cotton bales, a gin-house, and a mill full of corn.

The 102nd's right wing landed in Charleston on April 9 and marched northwest from April 11-13 to the Santee River, engaging enemy cavalry. On April 18 it also fought near Camden, thirty miles northeast of Columbia.

The left wing skirmished with Confederate forces at Spring Hill on April 16, and the next day, near Singleton's Plantation, flanked the Confederates and forced their retreat. The 102nd's fighting ended on

April 21 near Camden, where 200 Confederates attacked a company of the 102nd and were repulsed.

That day, news of the truce between Sherman and Confederate General Johnson reached the men of the 102nd, and the ceasefire took effect. Thus, some of the final shots of the Civil War were fired and received by the 102nd.

Powell's regiment returned to Charleston and was put on prison guard duty there until September 30, when it was mustered out of service. On October 17, 1865, the regiment returned to Detroit and disbanded.

In a year and a half of service, the 102nd saw 140 of its men die. Only eleven died of combat wounds, the rest victims of disease. While this might seem high by modern warfare standards, nearly 16% of soldiers in colored regiments died from diseases or accidents.

Little is known about Elijah Powell's personal involvement in his regiment's action. He was discharged when his regiment disbanded. According to his 1906 obituary, Powell "served so gallantly" that he rose to corporal and then sergeant of Company E.

Family, Barbering, Moving to Mishawaka

After the war, in 1866, Elijah married Mary Ann Hackley, the twenty-three year old daughter of Nancy and the late Reverend J.W. Hackley of Niles, Michigan. The Hackleys moved to Niles in 1850 from Chillicothe, Ohio, where Mary Ann was born. Reverend Hackley co-founded the Second Baptist Church in Niles in 1851.

The newlyweds' first child, Medora, was born in November 1866, and the family was listed in the 1867 South Bend city directory, residing at the corner of Marion and Sanger Streets, just northwest of the downtown. Farrow Powell's family also was still living in downtown South Bend.

Like many African American men in the nineteenth century, Elijah became a barber, following his older brother Colonel.

In the 1850 census, the most common trade for African Americans in Indiana towns was barber. Even by 1890, of the 2,287 African American men in Indiana with a skilled profession, the largest single group was barbers, with 699. The number of African Americans who were able to have a skilled trade was small in the nineteenth century. More were able to make a living as domestics or laborers. African Americans had been limited by discrimination, lack of skills and training, and hostile unions, which together account for why only 5% of their total population in Indiana had a skilled trade in 1890.

Barbering was a bright spot in the employment picture for African Americans, though, a profession that whites expected and accepted African Americans in. African American barbers who owned their own business contributed to the growth of a small African American middle class.

Barbers performed more services than just cutting hair and giving shaves. In African American communities, in particular, they functioned as doctors and dentists, gave out news and information, and sometimes even were bankers. The barber shop was one of the cornerstones of an African American community.

In 1867 Elijah Powell was a barber in South Bend. That he was not part of a large African American population is important; his business success had to come from serving mainly white customers. This would be a theme throughout the rest of Powell's personal and professional life: being part of a small African American population co-existing with a large white majority.

Elijah and Mary Ann moved to Mishawaka in 1868, residing on South Main Street, on the block where the Medical Arts Building stands today. Elijah's eighteen year old brother Benjamin boarded with the Powells, perhaps working with Elijah, whose shop was near the intersection of Main and Second Street (now Lincoln Way). The 1869 city directory listed only three barbers in Mishawaka: Elijah Powell, Joseph Heiser, and Mathew Sawyer, all of whom operated within a block of the Main-Second intersection. Sawyer also was African American.

Soon after their move to Mishawaka, the Powell family grew with the births of Emma in 1868, Frances in 1869, and William in 1871. The first tragedy in the married life of Elijah and Mary Ann Powell was William's death in September 1872.

Six more Powell children were born by 1878, although only Grace, Maud, and Herman lived to adulthood. The **Mishawaka Enterprise** did not fail to note, with some humor, the addition of each new family member. When a son was born in 1875, the **Enterprise** reported, "Lige Powell thinks he has a little barber now which will fill the bill. The little shaver arrived Sunday morning and weighed 9 1/2 lbs." When Herman was born in 1877, this theme continued: "Lige Powell smiles serenely as he manipulates the razor over his customers' faces, thinking in less than a score of years he will have that little shaver, which arrived on Wednesday, to assist him." These were prophetic words: Herman was a barber by 1900, and Elijah's other three sons followed.

Business must have been good for Elijah. He moved to a newly built basement shop at 103 North Main Street. Beginning in 1874 and running for thirty years, Powell had a small advertisement in the

On the way to his barber shop at 103 North Main Street, Elijah Powell would have walked down the 100 block of East Second Street in downtown Mishawaka, shown here c. 1900.

Mishawaka Enterprise. The text always read,

ELIJAH POWELL

Tonsorial artist, facial operator, physiognomical
hair dresser, cranium manipulator, and capillary abridger.

SHAVES AND CUTS HAIR

with ambidextrous facility.
He respectfully asks the patronage
of the citizens, and guarantees satisfaction.
Shop in basement of Beiger's block.

This ad informed customers what Powell could do for them and suggests a flair for language. **Tonsorial** refers to barbering. A barber who gives shaves would be a "facial operator," and cutting hair makes one a "cranium manipulator." **Physiognomical** deals with determining character traits from facial features, suggesting Powell's talent at matching hair style with personality. "Capillary abridger"-- one who shortens the capillaries-- indicates an effect of shaving or a haircut on the skin.

More Powells and Facing Loss

In 1880 a son, Jeremiah, was born, and the eight Powells continued to be at the center of the African American community in Mishawaka. Living next to them were Mary Ann's mother, Nancy, and Nancy's fifteen year old granddaughter. One more house away were three other African American women: a 43 year old mother and her nineteen and eleven year old daughters. They may also have been relatives. The mother's birthplace was Ohio, and the daughters were born in Michigan, a pattern reflecting Mary Ann Powell's own migration.

The Powells had three more children: Otto (1881), Elijah Eugene (1883), Farrow Raymond (1888). Again, the **Enterprise** took notice. When Otto was born, the newspaper commented, "Lige Powell received his annual contribution No. 12, on Sunday. It is a boy. If everybody obeyed the scriptural injunction as this family has done, Mishawaka would be a big city today." Elijah Eugene's birth brought this response: "Our colored population is rapidly increasing of late. Mrs. Elijah Powell added another son to the census last Friday." Farrow Raymond's birth led the **Enterprise** to say, "Elijah Powell claims the championship on babies. His wife on Wednesday presented him with his fourteenth child-- a big boy."

The 1880s also brought great sadness to the Powells as they experienced several deaths in their family. Benjamin, Elijah's brother, died in 1884, at age 34, and Farrow, Jr., died the next year at age 18. Farrow, Sr., followed his sons in death in 1887. The **South Bend Tribune** eulogized the Powell family patriarch: "Mr. Powell was frugal in his habits, a good manager and at all times a good citizen. He and his wife raised a large family of children, who, like him are good citizens and have the respect of all who knew him." In 1888 Mary Ann Powell's mother died "in full triumph of the faith," said the **Enterprise**. She had 81 grandchildren at the time.

In 1895 Elijah's step-mother, Rebecca, died, at age 71. The **South Bend Daily Times** noted that not all of her children were hers by birth; nonetheless, "she made no distinction; they all went to school, and received the same parental love and care." Her obituary describes her as both a "loving mother" and a "benefactor" of the community.

Elijah and Mary Ann also lost their twenty year old daughter Maud to typhoid in 1896.

In September 1902 Mary Ann Powell died after developing malaria. The **Enterprise** described her as "a well known and high esteemed citizen," "an earnest and consistent member of the First Christian Church," and "an exemplary wife, mother, and citizen."

After her death Elijah continued to live at 109 South Cedar with his four sons, all of whom were barbers. In 1903 the Powells' daughter Frances died, leaving behind three children in South Bend.

After suffering for several months with stomach cancer and then a stroke, Elijah Powell died on September 22, 1906, nearly 65 years old. According to the **Enterprise**, "he bore the respect and friendly opinion of the entire community." He was "one of Mishawaka's best known citizens and probably the oldest barber in continuous business in Northern Indiana," having barbered for nearly forty years. The

Elijah and Mary Ann Powell are buried in City Cemetery, South Bend.

Mishawaka paper also noted Elijah's record of valor in the army "was equaled by his record as a citizen." The **South Bend Tribune** eulogized Powell as "a brave soldier, a good citizen, a loving husband and father."

On the day of Powell's large funeral, most local barber shops closed in his honor. The Mishawaka and South Bend posts of the Grand Army of the Republic conducted services and provided pallbearers. Elijah Powell was buried next to his wife in South Bend's City Cemetery.

At the time of Elijah Powell's death, six of his children were alive: Medora, Grace, Herman, Otto, Elijah, and Farrow Raymond. Herman died in 1923. Elijah moved to Chicago around 1921 and died there in 1942. Medora died in 1931. Otto was a barber in Mishawaka for over sixty years, until his death in 1956. At that time, his sister Grace and brother Farrow Raymond were living in Chicago. Grace married, but her husband died in 1931. She died in 1963 at age 90; Grace and her husband are buried in Mishawaka's Fairview Cemetery, along with Medora, Herman, and Otto and his wife. Farrow Raymond died in 1974 and is buried in Chicago.

Elijah and Mary Ann Powell's legacy also includes several grandchildren and nearly 40 progeny now living across the United States. In addition to Frances' three children, Otto had two daughters and a son. Farrow Raymond had one son, and Elijah Eugene also had a son. Grace had no children, and Medora and Herman did not marry.

Elijah Powell's Place in History

Elijah's legacy and significance extend beyond his family and descendants. His life is a window into Mishawaka and Indiana before, during, and after the Civil War. He was a product of the great migration that took hundreds of thousands of African Americans and millions of their descendants from the rural South and often slavery to Northern farms and cities and the opportunities of the middle class. His occupation and his father's also typify the experience of many African Americans, beginning as tenant farmers or farm laborers, progressing to farm ownership and skilled trades like barbering.

Elijah was not unique as an African American barber; hundreds of others in Indiana followed his career path in the nineteenth century. What makes Powell noteworthy as a barber is that he conducted his business in an almost entirely white community. Many African American barbers in cities like Indianapolis worked, at least initially, in their own neighborhoods, serving people mainly of their own race. Elijah Powell, on the other hand, had to integrate himself into the community and be accepted by the white population. His longevity of service to Mishawaka, as well as his sons' involvement as barbers, reflects on these men as individuals, but also on their community and how it accepted African Americans-- at least in small numbers-- during a time when prejudice and nativism were prevalent.

Powell spent most of his life at the center of a small concentration of African Americans in Mishawaka and maintained ties with his South Bend family. Nonetheless, his life in Mishawaka-- even apart from barbering-- must have included some integration with the white community. Unlike South Bend, Mishawaka had no African Methodist Episcopal church for African Americans to gravitate to. Instead, Elijah and Mary Ann attended the First Christian Church, which stood downtown on West Second Street. Powell also was probably the only African American member of Mishawaka's Houghton Post of the Grand Army of the Republic. The Powells' obituaries speak of their community's high regard for them, esteem exceeding what would be given to someone seen merely as a service provider.

Elijah's children also show the family's integration into the community. In addition to the sons working as barbers in Mishawaka, two of Elijah's and Mary Ann's children stand out. Medora was the first African American graduate of Mishawaka High School. The **Mishawaka Enterprise** noted that her 1887 graduation was the first by an African American in northern Indiana. She later was a teacher and nationally prominent in African American women's social organi-

Farrow Raymond Powell, the second African American graduate of Mishawaka High School, also graduated from Fisk University in Nashville, Tennessee. He is shown here as a Fisk student, c. 1912.

zations. The only other Powell child to graduate from Mishawaka High was Farrow Raymond in 1908. The school's second African American graduate, he was also captain of the football team and a member of the basketball and track teams. Denied admission to the University of Notre Dame because of his race, Raymond later graduated from Fisk University and the Northwestern University Dental School and was a long-time dentist in Chicago.

The Powell family illustrates the philosophy of Booker T. Washington, the former slave and prominent civil rights leader of that era. Washington urged African Americans to lift themselves up by learning a skilled trade, working hard, and earning the respect of their white neighbors. Regardless of whether Elijah, Mary Ann, and their children ever consciously followed Washington's advice, they certainly lived, with great success, what he was teaching.

Elijah Powell is also significant for his role in the Civil War, sacrificing for African Americans' freedom and equality in the Union. While he was not required to go to war, he volunteered and then fought with distinction and led men in battle. Powell's participation in the war is part of an important chapter in American military and social history. Mishawaka's diversity was richer because Elijah brought his experiences from the war to his adopted community.

The Powells also reflect the social development of Mishawaka during the forty years after the Civil War. Their upward mobility and ownership of their home were a dream shared by their fellow townspeople, regardless of race or nationality. Like others in their time, the Powells took in under their roof aged relatives, young extended family, and others of their race who were starting out in a new town. In all of these ways, the Powells mirror thousands of Mishawaka families of diverse ethnic backgrounds.

Also important is Elijah Powell's vantage point on the development of Mishawaka. As one of only a handful of barbers in town, Powell would have served many of his townsmen, including influential men like Beiger, Jernegan, Dodge, and Perkins, who might have come to Powell's downtown shop to get the latest news of each other's activities and ventures. Elijah Powell would have had knowledge of the lives of

Mishawakans few others would have known. Powell also witnessed many changes and tremendous growth in Mishawaka, including the start of the transition from horse-drawn transportation to the automobiles sputtering by as he walked down Second Street to his basement barber shop.

Elijah Powell's role in his country and his community reminds us that seemingly ordinary lives, when examined closely, reveal much significance, even their own distinct greatness. Long departed from his Mishawaka, Elijah Powell speaks a message we can benefit from hearing.

CHAPTER 3

MEDORA POWELL:
BREAKING NEW GROUND
FOR AFRICAN AMERICANS

Born into a prominent local African American family, Medora Ann Powell became a pioneer in the history of Mishawaka High School and African American women in Indiana.

Powell was born in South Bend on November 13, 1866, the oldest of Elijah and Mary Ann Powell's fourteen children. Medora's father and uncles served in the Union army during the Civil War, and her paternal grandparents were among the first African American residents of St. Joseph County. Her maternal grandfather founded the Second Baptist Church in Niles, Michigan.

In 1868 the Powells moved to Mishawaka, where Medora spent much of her childhood. The family initially resided on South Main Street, near the site of the present-day Medical Arts Building. Medora's father, a barber in Mishawaka until his death in 1906, may then have been the longest continually practicing barber in northern Indiana.

In 1887 Medora Powell was the first African American to graduate from Mishawaka High School, one of ten graduates in her class.

According to the **Mishawaka Enterprise**, Medora was also the first African American graduate of any high school in northern Indiana.

The **Enterprise** of June 10, 1887, gave a detailed account of the high school's commencement, held at the opera house in the 100 block of West Second Street (today Lincoln Way). In reference to Medora, the paper stated, "Great interest centered in the appearance of this promising young pupil, not only from the fact that she is the first colored scholar ever graduated in northern Indiana, but because of her high standing as a pupil."

Each graduate of the Class of 1887 addressed the packed crowd of several hundred. Medora Powell's address was on the theme "Self Made Men." The **Enterprise** reported that her thesis was that self-educated men were not narrow-minded, giving examples of self-made men to prove that the "most noted and broadest minded men of the age virtually rose to eminence through their own exertions."

Two prominent examples Medora cited were the assassinated

Medora Ann Powell, the first African American graduate of Mishawaka High School, is shown here with the rest of the Class of 1887.

Powell and her classmates attended the old Mishawaka High School, located at Hill and First Streets.

President James A. Garfield and Frederick Douglass. She said Garfield had emerged from "obscurity and poverty" to become president, while Douglass overcame the even greater impediment of "brutal and cruel slavery itself."

The **Enterprise** noted, "The speaker's delivery was excellent, her manner clear and convincing. Round after round of applause rewarded her at the close of her effort."

Medora Powell would be the only African American graduate of Mishawaka High School for twenty years, until her brother Farrow Raymond in 1908. Medora's niece, Marie Moore, in later years described Medora as "ahead of her time" because of her schooling and the values taught by her family.

As an adult, Medora never married and lived most of her life in Mishawaka and South Bend. For at least a while, though, Medora was a teacher in Spencer, Terre Haute, and at Brownsville School in Cass County, Michigan. According to Powell family historian John Charles

Bryant, she may have been attracted by Michigan's easier licensing requirements for teachers and Cass County's sizable African American population. Medora left teaching and came back to Mishawaka to care for family members, perhaps after her sister Frances died and left young children behind.

Medora Powell was active in African American club and church activities in South Bend, and at the state and national levels.

From 1916-19, she was president of South Bend's St. Pierre Ruffin Club, which, according to a club publication of the time, was exclusively for African American women, "formed for the purpose of liberal culture and bringing together women with the view of rendering them helpful to each other and to society."

Medora also served as treasurer of the Olivet AME Church in South Bend, which her grandfather Farrow Powell helped establish in 1871. Through her church, she became South Bend's first Grand Matron of the Eastern Star for Indiana. Medora later traveled throughout the country and gained national prominence as grand treasurer of the national Order of the Eastern Star, a post she held for many years. Medora also served as treasurer of both the State Federation of Colored Women's Clubs and the local chapter of the NAACP. These treasurer positions reflect both Medora's business acumen and the Powell family's reputation for frugality.

Medora was also national president of the Ladies Confederate Club.

Owen Garner, whose wife was also a Grand Matron of the Eastern Star in Indiana, remembers Medora as "very quiet," "precise," and "educated."

Medora Powell lived most of her later years in her family's home at 109 South Cedar Street in Mishawaka, but moved permanently to South Bend around 1929. City directories from the 1920s list her as a maid and cook.

In June 1931 Medora, attending a conference of the Order of the Eastern Star in Jeffersonville, Indiana, suddenly took ill and died. She was buried in the family plot in Mishawaka's Fairview Cemetery. In the 1940s and 1950s, a local youth chapter of the Eastern Star was named for Medora Powell.

The Powell family was well known and highly regarded in Mishawaka for decades. They valued skilled trades and formal education, and this emphasis can be seen with Medora Powell. Medora also illustrates the high level of acceptance and integration of a small number of African Americans into Mishawaka, almost entirely a white community. She achieved her success alongside her white classmates, and, as the **Enterprise's** account suggests, her community expressed pride in Medora's accomplishments, like it would have for any son or daughter of Mishawaka.

As an adult, Medora reflected professions typically available for women in her time: teacher, cook, and maid. Like many of her women contemporaries, she found an outlet for her social and organizational talents through her church and clubs, making her mark in state and national offices.

More than 70 years after her death, Medora Powell remains a role model for successful racial integration and commitment to education, family, and community.

CHAPTER 4

PORTRAIT OF A COMMUNITY: AFRICAN AMERICANS IN MISHAWAKA IN 1900

At the turn of the twentieth century, Mishawaka had a small, but growing African American community. The 1900 census and city directories reveal much about these African Americans living in an almost entirely white community.

Twenty-one African Americans were residing in Mishawaka, out of a population of 5,560. While the African American population had increased from 19 in the 1890 census, its percentage of the overall population had fallen from .56% to .38%.

Most significant is the concentration of African Americans in 1900 within a few square blocks east of the downtown, an area bordered on the north by the St. Joseph River, Laurel Street to the east, Church Street to the west, and Fourth Street to the south. Eighteen of Mishawaka's twenty-one African Americans a century ago lived in seven different households in this neighborhood.

The main thoroughfare of this neighborhood was East Second Street (today Lincoln Way), home to the most influential Mishawaka families in 1900. While the African Americans living on this street probably did not interact with these families as socio-economic equals, they did live integrated with their white neighbors. No two African American households in Mishawaka in 1900 were next door to each other.

The closest African American to the downtown was twenty-five year old Lena Jeffries, a servant for Ed and Nellie Jernegan. The Jernegans resided at 221 East Second (today the site of the Mishawaka-Penn-Harris Public Library). Ed Jernegan was editor and publisher of the **Mishawaka Enterprise**.

Martin and Susie Beiger lived next door to the Jernegans at 215 East Second. Martin was president of the Mishawaka Woolen Manufacturing Company, known to generations of Mishawakans as Ball Band.

Across the street from the Jernegans lived Manuel Fisher and his wife Elizabeth. Manuel was elected Mishawaka's first mayor in 1899 and was also president of the Perkins Windmill and Ax Company. Their neighbor was James Roper, president of the Roper Furniture Company, another leading Mishawaka industry.

At 301 East Second lived Sarah Eberhart, widow of Adolphus Eberhart. He and Beiger founded Mishawaka Woolen.

The 400 block included several more prominent families. Living at 415 was Hattie Dodge, widow of Wallace Dodge, the founder of Dodge Manufacturing Company. Her neighbors were Otto and Martha Lang. Otto Lang owned a hardware store in the downtown. Both the Dodge and Lang homes remain today on Lincoln Way East, important links to this neighborhood's past. Melville Mix, president of Dodge Manufacturing Company and the Dodges' nephew, lived with his wife at 434 East Second.

Two other African Americans also were servants and resided with families on East Second Street. At 502 (today the site of the 500 High Rise) Grace Winburn lived with Ida Quigg, the widow of John Quigg, who had owned a downtown dry goods business. Two doors to the east, at 526, Lulu Winburn lived and worked for William and Claribel Orton. William was secretary of the Western Gas Engine Company and editor of **Power and Transmission**, a periodical published by

The Elijah Powell family home at 109 South Cedar Street was the center of the African American community in Mishawaka for many years.

Dodge Manufacturing Company. The Winburns were probably sisters; Grace was twenty and Lulu was twenty-six and divorced.

The Winburn sisters' neighbor was John Hollister, who lived at 518 East Second and owned a grocery store in the downtown. The Hollister house still stands on Lincoln Way East, another link to the neighborhood these African Americans and their white neighbors shared a century ago.

Just around the corner from the Ortons resided the most prominent African American family in Mishawaka. Elijah Powell, 58, and his wife Mary Ann, 56, lived at 109 South Cedar Street with four of their children: Herman, 22; Otto, 18; Eugene, 17; and Raymond, 12. Otto and Herman were barbers in their father's basement shop at 103 North Main Street. Also living with the Powells as a boarder was eighteen year old laborer Ellis Allen. The Powell house also still stands.

A half block to the east at 617 East Second lived two African Americans. Alonzo Pompey, 25, resided here with his white wife Katie

The home of John Hollister, 518 East Second Street, was a prominent land-mark in the neighborhood where most of Mishawaka's African Americans resided in 1900.

and Alonzo's twenty-two year old cousin, Lafayette Pompey. Alonzo and Lafayette drove ice wagons for William Scearce, who operated an ice house at 620 East Second, next to his home at 626.

Other African Americans resided just south of Second Street.

The Grady household at 212 South Union Street included five African Americans. Robert Grady, 49, was a barber at 104 East Second, and he lived with his wife Lola, 29, and fourteen-year-old son Clyde. Two boarders lived with the Gradys: Ollie Scott, 20, who also was a barber, and Lanford Hill, 30, a laborer.

Around the 300-400 block of East Fourth lived William Potter, 46, a widower with no occupation listed.

The only three African Americans in Mishawaka in 1900 not living in this neighborhood were at 802 West Fourth. Mary Grundy, a fifty-one year old widow, resided here with her son Joseph, 22, a day laborer. Day laborer Whitney Stuart, 45, was a boarder with the Grundys.

The census data for these 21 people further defines this African American community. Of this group, 14 had occupations listed. Five were barbers, three were domestic servants, four were day laborers, and two drove ice wagons. While the number of barbers is disproportionate for African American communities in Indiana at the time, it is consistent with barber being their most common skilled trade. In fact, in Mishawaka it was the only skilled trade for African Americans. Laborers and domestic servants were usually the most common occupations after barber, and Mishawaka's small sampling illustrates this.

Place of birth information is available for nineteen residents. Nine were born in Indiana, seven in Michigan, two in Ohio, and one in North Carolina.

This population was also quickly changing. Other than the Powells, none of the African Americans listed in the 1870 and 1880 censuses for Mishawaka was listed in 1900.

Of these families and households, three owned the home they lived in: the Powells, the Gradys, and Mary Grundy. All three were owned free of any mortgage.

The town's African American population, as a whole, had aged since the 1880 census. In 1880 the average age for Mishawaka African Americans was 18, but in 1900 it was 30. Elijah Powell was the oldest at 58, and his son Raymond was the youngest at 12.

The 1900 census also had questions about literacy, asking whether people could read and write. All the African Americans in Mishawaka except Mary Grundy and Whitney Stuart said they could both read and write.

A century later, the African American community in Mishawaka is larger and growing faster than at any time in the city's history. Mishawaka's African American population grew from 1.6% of the city's total in 1990 to 4.3% in 2000. This changing ethnic make-up will bring a host of challenges to Mishawaka in the years ahead. The successful integration of African Americans in Mishawaka a century ago offers a valuable model as the Princess City becomes more racially diverse in the twenty-first century.

CHAPTER 5

❖

GROWING UP IN MISHAWAKA: HELEN JERNEGAN DOOLITTLE REMEMBERS

Sledding down Race Street...tin-roof sundaes at The Melrose... streetcars on Lincoln Way. Some Mishawakans today may have heard about these experiences, but few remember firsthand these features of Princess City life in the 1910s and 1920s.

Lifelong Mishawaka resident Helen May Jernegan Doolittle recalls these events and many others from her childhood and adolescence. Born in 1910, Mrs. Doolittle has observed much change in her hometown and participated in some of the important events of twentieth-century American history. Her recollections give insight into the lives of children in Mishawaka between 1910 and 1927, as well as the challenges of the Depression and World War II.

In this oral history interview, Mrs. Doolittle shares some of these memories.

When and where were you born?

One-fifteen South Race Street is part of the library parking lot now.

*Helen Jernegan
Doolittle is shown here
in her 1927 Mishawaka
High School yearbook
photo and in 2000.*

That house was razed when they had brought in urban renewal, and my brother nearly had a stroke over it. He tried so hard to save it, and he went to all kinds of expense and everything else to curtail that, but they said, no, they needed it, and they took it. The house next door, the old Herzog house, was torn down, too, so that whole block is gone, but I was born there...February 3, 1910.

I had a brother older and a sister five years younger-- all three of us were born there. The doctor who delivered us lived right directly south one block in the house that Jim Davis has his dental office in. His name was Dr. Doan, and his wife, Dr. Anna Doan, was the dentist-- and the first woman dentist around here. So she was our dentist, and he was our doctor. Very convenient! Can you imagine that now? I grew up there-- I've been here all my life except for the times that I was in school and during the war when my husband was in service and I traveled around the country after him.

What was your childhood like?

I had a very very happy, uneventful childhood, really. I thought so many times about the freedom I had, that we all had as children growing up in a day when it was unheard of to have any horrible things like rape and murder and robbery and so forth that's going on today. My good friends that I used to pal around with when I was in Bingham School, where I went all through the grade school, we'd pack a little lunch and hike out to the woods-- the hills, we called it-- south of Mishawaka, which is now all built up: Blair Hills. We spent the day out there, picking violets and just doing all kinds of things in the woods. Our parents never worried about us. They knew we were out there, but they never said be careful or anything. We trotted back home and never thought a thing about it. We played in the streets. Of course, there weren't automobiles then like there are today. I was a tomboy. I played football and baseball in the streets with the boys. There were very few girls in my neighborhood, so I grew up with boys, and I preferred boys. I think I did all my life.

I remember that we had a music teacher at Bingham School by the name of Winifred Wunderlich. People around here still remember her. She's since gone. She instigated a music program in which we would listen to records of mostly classical music for a whole semester, and at the end of that semester we had what we called a music memory contest for all the schools in Mishawaka-- grade schools. I remember one in particular was held over at Battell School, and I remember going to that one. It was in the summer, and I won the one I was in, and I got a ten-dollar gold piece. I was so proud of that. Today that wouldn't mean anything. That was one of my fond memories, and I remember Winifred Wunderlich so much because she was a wonderful teacher.

But then, we had to go down to the Main Junior High School, which at that time was right directly north of the present old high school that is now the furniture store. I went to school there. We had as our principal Pappy Moran. His name was Claude Moran, and his wife was Maude Moran. They both came from Osceola, and he was the most wonderful philosopher. I always remember one thing he taught us all, every class: to remember that initiative is doing the right thing at the right time at the right place without being told. And I still remember. We all loved him so. He lived to be quite old-- I don't remember-- he's-- both of them gone, but I don't think too long ago. I think their home in Osceola was given to the town. I think they made it into a library, the Moran house.

When I had my first two-wheeler bike, I used to bike all the way down to the new high school, 'cause they had that great big wide sidewalk in front, and we'd ride our bicycles up and down there, and then come on back home.

When I was in high school, I got twenty-five cents a week for my allowance. We had trolleys in those days, interurbans-- or whatever you want to call them. Streetcars going right down Lincoln Way, and I could ride that to school for a nickel, but I saved that. I walked instead because I wanted to save those nickels, and at the end of the week, I went down to The Melrose in Mishawaka, which was located on east Lincoln Way on the south side, and I got a tin roof for ten cents. That was ice cream with chocolate sauce and peanuts.

The Herzog home, Mr. Herzog had a cleaning and tailoring shop on Church Street right across from where the library is now. They lived right next door to us, but there was also at some time or other a Coats Funeral Home, and I can remember as a little girl, I would go over across the yard and peak into the basement windows of that house where they kept the caskets, thinking maybe we'd see a dead body and all. I remember that so clearly. Then they moved. The Coats Funeral Home moved over on Lincoln Way on the corner of Race Street and Lincoln Way East on the north corner. Now that since has been a Ziker's Cleaner. So I don't remember whether the Herzogs built that house and then moved out of it or what. But they were our neighbors.

Then across the street were the Beymons. They moved to California. John was their only child. He's died since.

North was A.D. Warner and that lovely brick home, and he was president of Mishawaka Rubber and Woolen-- the Ball Band, we called it then.

Next door to the west of [the Jernegans] was the Higgins home. That was the first home of Susie Beiger. Her name was Higgins, and when she was married then, of course, she married Martin Beiger, and they started building that home on Lincoln Way, Union Street. That was next to my grandfather's home.

Then, when I came along, I think there was the Mohler Drug Store that was in there and also the Tribune. Oh gosh, this is taking me back.

On the corner was Marie Towle-- and they had this huge back yard that went all the way almost to where the post office was then. As kids, we'd go over there-- and my parents knew it-- we would dig tunnels in her back yard, and, bless her heart, she never complained, and we'd take potatoes down underneath in that tunnel and bake them. Now, we had fire underneath there! Can you imagine parents today letting their kids do that? They'd be scared to death. We'd bake those potatoes, and we thought that was wonderful. Oh boy, those potatoes tasted so good. That was Marie Towle. I remember her. That was on the corner.

All those buildings are gone. Just think of it-- all library now. It's nice to grow old and yet it isn't.

Right next door to the Herzog house on Third Street were the Cuffberg Apartments, and that was quite a large home. There were quite a few apartments there. Oh, little by little, I think of things, but I jump around, don't I?

One more thing I did want to tell you: Maggie Prickett, who was Maggie Harris, lived a couple blocks from me on Lincoln Way East, and she was also a tomboy, and she was just about a year older than I. She and I used to play together, and we were kind of devilish...One time, I remember particular, we got hold of some little straight pins and we went over to the corner of Race and Lincoln Way and waited till we knew that there was a streetcar coming, and we laid the pins on the streetcar tracks and waited till they went by, and then we went over and salvaged what was left, and we thought that was so smart because they were all smashed and looked like little swords.

My great-grandfather [Jernegan] started the **Enterprise**. His father was a printer in LaPorte, Indiana, and he took his printing business over to Michigan City and developed a newspaper. My grandfather Ed

The Edward Jernegan home was located at 221 East Second Street, shown here c. 1903. Ed Jernegan was Helen Jernegan Doolittle's grandfather and the publisher of the Mishawaka Enterprise.

Mishawakans showed their patriotism and community spirit through street parades like this one, c. 1909.

Jernegan then published the newspaper when he was older, but he was in the Civil War as a drummer boy and was too young to serve in the-- had to leave and reenlisted.

My one memory of my grandfather was that he had had a stroke before he died, and he lived in the apartment building that was on the corner there that was torn down. They had the big cupola bay window. I remember him sitting in that room in his wheelchair with his little flag waving it, and they brought the parade-- they called it Armistice Day then-- down around that corner so that Grandpa could see them. The tears just rolled down his cheeks—he couldn't talk—and he waved that flag because it meant so much to him that they had honored him that way.

Grandpa loved to write, and he kept a journal of my grandmother Jernegan's malaprops. She always got words a little mixed up. One of the funny stories we've always told about her was that she was an ardent Episcopalian and she was a member of the church in

Mishawaka and went to church regularly, and she tried to get my grandfather to attend with her. Once in a while he would, but he wasn't as gung ho about it as she was. So one Sunday she couldn't get him to go. She trotted out the side door of the home, and as she got out in front, she turned around and just yelled right back at Grandpa, "I'm the only damned Christian in this family!" and trotted on down. My grandfather thought that was so funny that he put that in his journal along with a lot of his other things. He thought she was so funny, and she was. She was real funny.

My father was Ralph Hartwell Jernegan, and my mother was Estella May Frank Jernegan, and her father was mayor of Mishawaka at one time. That was before my time. His family had come from Pennsylvania and settled in Woodland, Indiana, to be in the lumber business. He also taught school, and so when they moved to Mishawaka later on when my mother was nine years old, Grandpa Frank came to Mishawaka and taught school here, and Mother met my father when she first entered school. They knew each other all through their life.

I had just the one brother, Paul Jernegan. He was a little over two years older than I. Then my sister is five years younger. My sister's name is Ruth Ann Runquist.

My father graduated from law school at the University of Michigan, and my mother after she graduated from high school-- as they did in those days-- she taught at Battell School, and then she taught one year at what they called then the orphans' home, which is now the Family and Children's Center. She taught there a year, and then-- she had musical aspirations. She sang and played the piano-- she went to the New England Conservatory in Boston for one year. Her father took her out there on the train when she first matriculated, and on the way they stopped in Buffalo over night, and that was the night that McKinley was killed [in Buffalo]. She was there a year, and then she came home and my father graduated. In those days, law school was three years, and Dad was ready to practice law. They were married in 1904. That's when they built that house next to the family home-- as they did in those days. Then my brother was born in 1908 and I was born in 1910 and my sister was born in 1915.

What is your earliest memory?

My earliest memory...was Christmas in our house. We had a three-story house on Race Street. The third floor was our play room, and all of our toys and everything were up there, and on Christmas Eve, after my folks went to church-- well, we were in bed-- they put the Christmas tree up. They carried that Christmas tree up two flights of stairs, up in the attic-- the third floor-- and decorated it. All of our gifts were put up there. We never saw a gift or anything until Christmas morning, and we never heard them going up to do all that. Isn't that something? I've thought of it so many times. That was the earliest memory, and I can remember the doll I got. It was given to me by Mrs. A.D. Warner, who lived right across the street. Now, that house was torn down, where Mel Hibschman had his filling station. That was a beautiful red brick house, and they tore that down. I remember Mrs. Warner always went to Chicago to Marshall Field's to do her Christmas shopping, and she brought me this doll, and I remember that doll so well. I think maybe that might have been one of my first memories. It's hard for me to go back that far...probably about four years old maybe. Gosh, if I had been any older, I probably would have heard them, but I never heard them.

What kinds of things did you enjoy doing the most in your childhood?

I enjoyed just playing. I had a lot of fun, just playing games. There was a boy who lived across the street from us by the name of John Beymon. They owned that house that sits on the corner of Race and Third Street, which was an Eberhart home originally. John was one of my playmates. We played baseball. I don't know whether we played football then or not-- I can't remember. We played Run-Sheepie-Run. I'm trying to think of all the games we played-- usually as a group in the neighborhood, usually early in the evening. Of course, at birthday parties-- pin the tail on the donkey and that sort of thing. We always had a big birthday party, and I remember also we had a lot of popcorn parties. Mothers would pop popcorn, and we'd sit out on our front porches. It's all very corny stuff now. As I say, we were so naive that our pleasures were very simple.

I went to the Presbyterian Church, and I went to Sunday School there every Sunday. My mother was the choir director there in church, and I used to go over and sit in the sanctuary while she had choir practice. The first Presbyterian Church was down on Lincoln Way West in Mishawaka originally, and that's where my mother was originally a member. When they built that new church-- the cornerstone is dated 1911, and I was baptized-- I was one of the first two babies baptized in that church by Dr. Horace Cady Wilson-- I remember his name.

What other memories do you have of Mishawaka when you were growing up?

What I remember about it is that we had what we called a Rubber-re, which was the Ball Band. They were making rubber boots in those days, and we had the awful smell that permeated everything-- all over. We got to the point where we didn't notice it so much, but I always remember how dirty everything was-- just filthy. You'd clean a window sill and a half hour later, it'd be full of soot again. We don't appreciate how much anti-pollutants we have enjoyed in recent years because that was awful. I remember Rubber-re, and I always remember mainly the Belgian population here, which was one of the best groups of people we had in Mishawaka.

My brother used to like to take his tricycle and take it down the hill on Race Street-- right straight down to the race, and one day somebody called my folks. They said, "Your son is riding his bicycle on the edge of that race," and my father called the police department, and at that time they had a big policeman they called Big Bill Turbush. Big Bill Turbush had every kid in town scared to death, and Dad knew that if Big Bill Turbush got down there that Paul would jump off his bike right now...and he did. He got him home-- Big Bill Turbush. But that hill-- Race Street-- which is still there-- we did all of our winter sliding there. My dad took us down there to slide, and we'd go all the way down to the very end. I learned to belly-flop-- do everything with the boys! Of course, they don't do that anymore.

When you were growing up, were times better or worse than for children growing up today?

Oh, when I was growing up, they were so much better. We didn't know as much.

We didn't have the knowledge that we have today. We weren't exposed to the world news and that sort of thing, but we had an appreciation of our environment, of our families. We respected our elders. We never would have thought of-- well, if we did, we certainly would have heard about it. We never sassed our teachers. If anything ever happened in school that my folks heard about, the teacher was right and I was wrong-- always. I got the punishment, and I was pretty bad in those days. I did a lot of whispering, talking, and passing notes and that sort of thing. Of course, that was the worst we did those days. I'm an old lady, and I don't like all that's going on today, and I suppose that when I was young, the older people didn't like what we were doing. I think of what Socrates said once. He said that the world was going to hell and back in those days, so I suppose that's going to be repeated. Here I was able to go all over any place without fear of being hurt, of being kidnapped, of being anything. But this was a small town, and maybe in the larger towns like Chicago, New York, it was happening more. I think we were more naive. I know I've learned so much from my grandchildren about things I never heard of, but I must have been very naive. I'm sure of that.

My family always had dinner together. Nowadays families don't eat together, which is too bad. We always had an argument at the dining room table, and we'd take a different side, which was probably my father's fault because he, being a lawyer, liked adversaries, and we'd all sit and argue something. We'd never get mad, but we'd just argue. Well, when I first had my future husband come for dinner at our house, he didn't like it. He couldn't get over it. He says, "All you do is argue. What do you want to argue all the time about?" He wasn't used to that, you know. This friend of mine, Ruth Munsee, used to come over to eat with us. She was with us a lot. She said, "Oh, it's more fun to go to the Jernegans 'cause they had so much fun at the dinner table." And we did. My mother didn't so much; she was kind of quiet. But the rest of us-- boy!

During your teenage years, what did you do to socialize with your friends?

Well, most of our social life was centered around the functions in high school. We had the usual things-- dances, games, football games. I remember one football game. One of my boy friends that I liked so well-- his name was Don Rodgers-- he played on the football team, and we played Central High School out at Notre Dame. I was there rooting for him, and he made the winning touchdown. Boy, was that great!

We had the usual high school things that we did. I remember going to one of the dances in high school, and I didn't have a date until the boy living on the block next to me by the name of Alan Laidlaw asked me to go to the dance. I didn't like him, but he asked me to go, and my mother said I had to go because the families were friends. I had my first pair of black satin shoes for the dance, and we walked to the high school because he didn't drive. Nobody drove in those days. We walked all the way up there, and the dance was in the gym. The dance started and he didn't know how to dance. He didn't even know how to take a hold of a girl to dance with her. I said, "You mean to say you can't dance?" Well, he tried, the poor guy. He was so embarrassed, but his folks had probably made him come, too. I got mad, and I walked out and walked home-- left him there. I think that was one of my first dates. My mother had a fit when I walked in and my shoes were ruined.

We used to have a lot of pep sessions. Now that's where Maggie Prickett came in. She was a cheerleader always.

And then we had a flagpole out in front of the high school, and I remember we used to climb that pole, skinny up, and do some cheering up there on the pole.

I wasn't particularly athletic, and I followed the football team because of Don, but that was the only reason I was interested. And basketball. I skipped school when I was, I think, a junior or senior in high school with another couple, and we drove all the way up-- that was when one guy had a car-- to-- Gosh, I think it was St. Joe. When we got back, my mother was standing out in front of the house because they had called from school to report that I wasn't in class. Boy, did I get it.

Would you consider Mishawaka when you were growing up to be a good place to live?

Oh yes, there was a great deal of civic pride. Yes, we had wonderful civic leaders. My memory of the main mayor was Mayor Ralph Gaylor, and my father was city attorney under him, so that's the reason I probably remember him more than any other. Then, there was Mason Petro. The golf course was named after him, and my father was instrumental in getting that 18th hole built with WPA because Dad was a golfer and he thought we ought to have more than a nine-hole golf course. He was very fond of Mason Petro. My family was rock-ribbed Republican, and Mason Petro was Democrat, but that's all right. He was a good mayor. At that time, really, I don't think there was that much difference between parties, as far as the mayor was concerned. I can remember when Spence Walton was elected mayor the first time, and my father met him on the street, and he said, "Spence, let me be the first person who didn't vote for you to congratulate you." It was that atmosphere always.

What are some memories you have of historical events when you were growing up? Do you remember World War I?

Well, yes, I do. That's when I learned to knit. My mother was knitting socks and things for the boys in service. They had a sewing group from our church. Some of the time they met at our house, and some time we'd go over to church, and I was taught to knit. Then my mother used to make-- my mother was a good cook-- she made real good egg noodles-- and she'd slice them very, very, very fine, and all her friends raved about her noodles. So they asked her to make up packages of noodles to send to the boys in service. Now I don't know how they managed to cook 'em, but she sent them in packages.

Then I remember Armistice. My dad was in the Home Guard. He was too old to be drafted and had a family, so he was in the Home Guard. I don't know exactly what they did. I think they marched. Dad got us all out of bed, and I can remember his putting me on his shoulders and we walked downtown to the middle of Mishawaka, and the band was out and everybody was out, waving flags. That was the 11th of November. Boy, did they celebrate! We all were so happy to have that war over, but it was too bad it didn't last.

I remember when Wilson was elected my father was so much against him, because Wilson had promised to keep us out of war, and we got into war. He wanted the League of Nations. He was ahead of his time on that one, Wilson was.

I was in college when Hoover was defeated-- that's right. I thought it was terrible, terrible. Franklin Roosevelt-- oh, yeah. When I went to work with the Department of Public Welfare, when I first started, the township trustee was handling all the welfare money, but it got to be so big they couldn't handle it. So, it was turned over to the state, and that's when I went to work for the Department of Public Welfare and not the township trustee. Well, the change in people's attitude towards taking relief, we called it then, was dramatic. Over night, when Roosevelt said we were going to take care of the forgotten man, everybody and his little brother who was out of work and thought he was deserving of help came in demanding-- not asking-- demanding. I used to get very upset, and I always blamed Roosevelt for that.

But looking back now and thinking of what he had in mind at the time, although he was a great politician, he still was doing probably the humanitarian thing because people were in terrible straits. I can remember having to ask children of indigent parents-- to tell the children, grown children, married children, "You have to take care of your parents. We cannot give them welfare as long as you are able to financially take care of them." Well, a lot of these young people were having a hard time taking care of themselves, but at that time that was the rule. I think back now and think how cruel that really was because it put the parents in a bad position.

I remember I had one man; his name was Harding-- I've forgotten his first name. I used to have an office out of Stuckey School in Clay Township on one day a week when I gave out welfare checks to the people living around Notre Dame, and they had a lot of them out there. This one man, I had gotten him a job at Bendix. That's what I did-- I tried to get people work. I got him a job, and he refused to take it. So when I found out about it-- he came in that next week asking for his welfare check, and I said, "No, I'm not going to give it to you." Of course, that was dumb, and I was so young and naive. I said, "No, I'm not going to give you that. You don't deserve it. If you don't want to work, then you don't deserve to be cared for." Well, he got mad and he pulled out a gun. Fortunately, I had a couple of policemen out there, from the sheriff's department, surrounding the school because they did that in those days, and the guy shot the policeman, and he was sent to prison for 10 years. Fortunately, I wasn't involved in the lawsuit, but I was always worried for fear he was gonna come at me someday, so I changed my name: I got married! But that was so dumb of me. I should have just given him the check and said, "Compliments of FDR." But I thought I was teaching him a lesson. Oh, dear...

Do you have memories of Pearl Harbor Day? Where were you?

Oh, sure. My husband was in the air force, and he had been in the reserves. He came out of college in 1929, and he went right into the air force because he thought that was going to be the future of America. He wanted to get into the aeronautics, so he became a pilot. Just at the time that he got his wings, they reduced the air force, and his whole group was put on reserve. He was in the reserves from that time on-- although he went to camp every summer for three weeks. Anyway, he was called back when they knew we were going to get back in the war, and that was the last of November of '41. I just had my second baby, but my folks had a place in Bayview, where they went every summer. So Bob took off. He had to go to Albany, Georgia, where they were setting up Turner Field to be a training camp for pilots to train for combat. Bob was ordered to be down there, so I went up to Bayview with my kids, stayed with my parents. Bob went down to Georgia and said he'd send for me whenever he had the chance, and at that time they said he'd be gone a year, so the government packed up all of our furniture and shipped it down to Albany. Bob had rented a house down there, and I got down there probably the end of November. Bob was on duty at Turner Field. He had a combat unit that he was training.

On Sundays, he'd take us all out for a drive. We were out on a little drive around the country, and we had a radio on in the car, and we heard that Pearl Harbor had been bombed. Immediately, they said, all military personnel report to the field-- immediately. Bob didn't have his uniform on, so he took us back to our house, and he said, "I don't know when I'll see you." He took off and went out to the field. Oh, so many of the officers out there had already served at Pearl Harbor and had a lot of their buddies there. Oh, they were just in hysterics almost until they assessed what had happened. I'll never forget Pearl Harbor Day, no.

Then Bob stayed there until he was sent to Clovis, New Mexico, to train on B-24s, and I was left in Albany with two little kids, and I didn't know what the heck to do with myself. I didn't know when he was going to be back or anything. I stayed there. He flew in to the base one time, and when I saw that great big bomber coming in, I thought, "You know, that thing's too big to fly." I never saw such a big ship in my life.

Anyway, I came back home. I got my house back; we lived at 414 North Wenger, and we'd had a tenant in our house. But I had my furniture brought back, and I went back to home and with my kids. Bob went out to Blythe, California, on another training mission.

Finally, he thought he was going to stay there a while so he sent for us, and I took a train from Mishawaka when the New York Central was still running in Mishawaka. They weren't serving meals during the war. Mother packed me a basket of food, and I got a bedroom, they called it. It was a compartment with upper and lower bunks. It took us three days to get to Los Angeles, and when I got there, Bob had an aunt living in Glendale. She met us, and when Bob came down from Blythe-- Blythe is in the southern tip of California, but it was just a short trip to Los Angeles. We went back to Blythe, and, oh, it was the hottest summer I ever put in. It's desert, you know.

He got orders to go to Walla Walla, Washington, so we packed up and drove all the way up to Walla Walla, Washington-- all the way up the coast. I can remember driving along the Columbia River Gorge, and it was the most beautiful-- that river is just gorgeous. We stayed there in a hotel overnight, and we were the only people in that hotel along the Columbia River. Of course, this is during war; people weren't traveling around. There was gas rationing for one thing. Anyhow, we ended up in Walla Walla, Washington.

We were there until Bob got orders to go to Tonapah, Nevada. We went to Tonapah, which is a very high elevation, an old silver mining town. Bob at that time was in charge of the base, and he had to figure out a way to feed the people. So they decided to bake their own bread. Bob was pretty good at food; he earned his way through college working in a kitchen and cooking. He had them bake bread, and the bread blew up because of the altitude. I always remember that.

We were there for a little while. They were training pilots for desert warfare, and the guys were being killed right and left in that area. Bob always said that it was the worst place that they could have been trained. We heard a lot of crashes out there; we lived on the base. It was pretty bad.

From Tonapah, he was sent to Murat, California, which is Edwards Air Force Base now. We lived on the base for about two months, and then he got his overseas orders. All this time, traveling around the United States, so he took us home, and he was there about two days and took off.

He ended up in Australia, and he was there a year. He was on the evaluation of something-or-other air force team. He didn't get into combat, thank heaven. He was too old for combat. So I was glad of that.

We had had a real estate business here, which he had had to leave.

When he came back, he had to start in all over. But he started his business again and kept it until our son Rick graduated from college, and he went into the business and took it over from his dad.

I was one of thousands of women that were doing the same thing at that time, and so many of them-- we were on bases where there were young people with the guys that were learning to flying and they'd be killed. Oh, it was sad, these young gals left alone.

CHAPTER 6

MEMORY'S VISION: REFLECTIONS ON THE LIFE OF PETER AMBROSE DE KEVER 1903-1965

I often wonder about what happens to us when we die. Biology explains how our bodies decompose, and religions offer interpretations of what happens to the soul. More intriguing, though, is what happens to our memory after we die. What endures as a reminder or memorial of our existence, a testament that once, for a brief time, we walked the earth?

When I think about how we live on, I think about my grandfather, Peter Ambrose De Kever, who died nearly three years before I was born. Although I never met him, he lives on in me through my name, my family, many photographs, and a few seconds of him walking and talking in a soundless Super-8 movie. Yet my grandfather lives most vividly in memories and stories about his life. For as long as I can remember, my father, Joe De Kever, has passed on to me these fragments of my grandfather's life, which have been added to by his friends, family, and co-workers. Photos provide a record of what my grandfather looked like, but these stories make the real portrait of the man, adding more detail and rich texture. Collecting and re-presenting those fragments of his life allows Grandpa to live again.

Childhood

Pete was born on January 20, 1903, in Beveren-Waes, Belgium, ten miles west of Antwerp. He was the second child and first son of Joseph and Leonie De Kever. My dad said Grandpa had no memories of the old country, but did have a vague recollection of making the Antwerp-New York transit in 1908, most likely in steerage on a passenger liner. It is not surprising that he would remember crossing the Atlantic, for there could have been no greater adventure for a poor boy growing up in a small Flemish town. Changes in the economic conditions in Flanders and the perception of economic opportunities in America had created a surge in immigration from Flanders to industrial cities in the

Peter Ambrose De Kever was born in Beveren, Belgium, on January 20, 1903. The De Kevers would have known St. Martin's Church, in the town center. It is shown here in 1990.

The De Kever family had this photo taken shortly after they were reunited in Mishawaka. Joseph had immigrated to the United States in 1904, and his wife Leonie and children Anna, Pete, and Elizabeth followed in 1908.

United States. Grandpa's family, like thousands of others, came to Mishawaka and settled in the Belgian West End.

Joseph De Kever died of typhoid in March 1912, leaving behind six children. At the time, the family was living in a small house at 422 Wells Street, alongside the railroad tracks near downtown. My grandfather kept vigil when Joseph's coffin was in their home. One night when a thunderstorm blew through town, Pete slept underneath the coffin, mourning and finding comfort from the storm by being close to his dead father.

Another of Pete's boyhood memories has been retold by my father. Great-grandmother De Kever told Grandpa that demons lived under the beds of boys who were bad, and one night, his mother asked a family friend to wait under the bed to scare him. As Grandpa lay on his bed, he felt something pushing up on his mattress from beneath, so he started throwing shoes at whatever was under the bed. "I always thought it really wasn't a case of him being afraid of the devil moreso than it was knowing that it was a human and teaching the guy a lesson. He was just showing that he wasn't afraid of anybody trying to scare him. He wasn't afraid of anything," Joe De Kever explained.

There is a lot that we do not know about my grandfather's youth, things he never shared with my dad. Pete did not attend high school, which was often the case with people of his generation. He may not even have completed St. Bavo School. According to my father, Grandpa may not have always been well behaved in school. In an era when every desk had an inkwell, "he would take the girl's pigtail and dip it into his inkwell."

His brother Achiel said that Pete left Mishawaka at age sixteen because "Papa" Schaut, whom Leonie had married in 1919, threw him out. Achiel says Schaut was mean to all of the family. It was this abusive atmosphere that Grandpa left when he began his years away from home.

Wayne Linson was a co-worker of my grandfather at Major Brothers meatpacking in the early 1940s. He and Pete grew close in their three years together at the slaughterhouse and often talked about Grandpa's experiences. Linson offered valuable insight on the period from when Pete left Mishawaka through his years at Major's.

Grandpa told Linson a different version of how he left Mishawaka. Linson remembered Pete said he was "sick and tired of everything" at home. "He had had a hard life at home and to hell with it. He left. There aren't too many people who'd have the guts to do that," Linson recalled. One day when Schaut gave him some change to get a gallon of milk, Grandpa just left and never came back. When he finally did return, a decade later, Schaut immediately asked where the milk and his change were.

By age sixteen, my grandfather was not only an adventurer but also a refugee from his own home. This gave him the opportunity to travel and to find his identity, his place in the world. Pete seized that chance and made the best of a bad situation.

Vagabond

My father felt Grandpa "really lived when he was young," and Wayne Linson frequently heard about Pete's experiences from this period, including threshing wheat, perhaps in North Dakota, and picking sugar beats, possibly in Kansas, with other Belgians. "He roamed around," Linson said, but Grandpa worked wherever he went: "He didn't have a lazy bone in his body." Pete told him that the field work of a migrant laborer was hard. For a young man seeking freedom, though, it must have been an enjoyable life.

Pete spent some of the 1920s and perhaps mid-'30s living on the bum in the Northwest and California. When my parents and sister were traveling in the San Francisco area, my dad recognized places that Grandpa mentioned when recounting his adventures. Grandpa later confessed that there were times when he was a hobo that, if he was hungry and saw a fresh-baked pie cooling on a window sill, he would take the pie. Life as a drifter has never been easy or safe, and my father suggested Pete was in situations where, in self-defense, he may have killed people. At some point he was shot and carried a bullet in his arm for the rest of his life. "I think he got it when he was on the bum somewhere," Joe De Kever explained. Grandpa also would tie himself to the boards underneath railroad boxcars and then ride the rails throughout the Pacific Northwest, untying himself and getting off when he chose. Somehow, he grew accustomed to traveling, let alone sleeping, just a couple feet above the ground, moving at sixty miles an hour. Like other hobos, Grandpa supported himself through odd jobs, which must have added to his diverse knowledge and experience.

Pete's years in the Midwest and the West Coast can be seen in a different light, considering Achiel's suggestion that Joseph De Kever was not one to stay in the same place for long. After all, in the span of a few years, the family had moved from Beveren to nearby Melsele, and then Joseph went to Norway, Michigan, and finally to Mishawaka by 1906. Achiel felt his father would have eventually ended up in California. Perhaps Grandpa's later travels to the Golden State and the West Coast were a fulfillment of his father's wanderlust.

After Pete left Mishawaka and before he went into the army, he spent time on freighters. He went to the Orient on a tramp steamer, and Achiel remembered that Grandpa was on the Yangtze River, one of China's great rivers and trade routes. Wayne Linson said Pete was always "interested in ships" and taking trips. Grandpa described the freighters he served on as "'trashy'" and noted the bad food and seasickness, but said, "'The money was always good.'" Linson said Pete was especially impressed by the Panama Canal and the big freighters moving through the locks and felt everyone should see that. Linson remembered Grandpa speaking with a tremendous knowledge of geography: "He was a world traveler...That man could talk about South America, he could talk about the United States, he could talk about the Orient."

Pete also picked up the culture that came with life on the freighters. Linson remembered his friend had "tattoos everywhere," which he noted were from Grandpa's merchant marine days because sailors are "tattoo people." Pete had snakes and other animals up and down his arms. When Linson once asked him how he got the snake tattoos, Grandpa merely replied, "'That's a long story,'" but Linson hinted alcohol may have played a role. My dad remembered his father also had a tattoo of the Blessed Virgin.

Sixty years after they worked together, Linson marveled at these years of Pete's life: "You gotta give that guy credit for everything he did because that took so much nerve." When asked how he did all those things, Pete responded dismissively, "'Ahhh!'" Linson added, "So all them kinds of things makes you wonder that a young man like that with no schooling could go out and do all them things and still come out with good character."

"Army Pete"

Pete was in the army from 1928-1934, an experience that caused Linson and other workers at Major's to refer to Grandpa as "Army Pete." My dad felt life in the army did much to settle Grandpa down. Not long after his discharge, Pete was back in Mishawaka and married my grandmother, Elsie Janssens, in 1938.

Grandpa's enlistment records provide some details of his army life. He enlisted on February 13, 1928, at the Presidio, in San Francisco.

His vocation was listed as truck driver. He was 25 years old, had blue eyes, light brown hair, a "ruddy" complexion, and stood 5' 8 1/2" tall. His birthplace was recorded as Mishawaka, so the army assumed he was an American citizen, but only in 1939 did he get a naturalization certificate. On September 7, 1929, Peter was promoted to corporal of the service battery of the 11th Field Artillery, stationed at Schofield Barracks, Hawaii. He completed his first tour of three years and was discharged at Fort McDowell, California, on March 3, 1931. When discharged, Grandpa's character was described as "excellent" and his physical condition "good."

Insight into Pete's life in the field artillery comes from Ralph J. Hillman, who served in the 11th Field Artillery beginning in 1935. Grandpa's service battery maintained the guns and vehicles of the regiment. Hillman said that gun carriages then were mounted on wooden wheels with iron rims which frequently popped off the wheels. Men in

Pete De Kever served in the United States Army from 1928-1934.

the service battery did not look kindly on the soldiers in the other batteries because they were often damaging the equipment. "Service batteries had no love for the guys like me who drove the trucks (and wrecked them) and sometimes dumped the entire truck and gun into a gulch...They would barely speak to us," Hillman wrote. Pay was $21 a month, but expenses from the canteen had to come out of that, Hillman noted, "so if you walked away from the pay table with $10 you were in good shape for another month." Soldiers from the 11th had liberty in Honolulu, which they could get to by a narrow-gauge railroad for $1. The men in artillery regiments wore knee-high leather boots, a carry-over from the days of horse-drawn artillery.

In March 1931 Pete re-enlisted at Fort Benjamin Harrison in Indianapolis and earned a $50 re-enlistment bonus. He served in the 3rd Field Artillery and possibly the 11th Infantry and was discharged at Fort Harrison in 1934. Grandpa was listed as a marksman with a rifle, was in good physical condition, and again had "excellent" character and "satisfactory" efficiency. His discharge papers in both 1931 and 1934 list Pete as a private, even though he had been promoted to corporal in 1929. Hillman gave an explanation for the change in rank. As a sergeant, Hillman lost a stripe when he went from Hawaii back to the mainland. Any promotion my grandfather had while at Schofield Barracks may similarly have been lost when he left Hawaii.

Life in the army would have offered Pete many interesting experiences, most of which, though, have been lost to us. Grandpa also did guard duty at the military prison on Alcatraz, within sight of the Presidio.

Back Home Again

Sometime after his discharge in 1934, Pete chose to settle down in the West End Belgiantown. His family knew my grandmother's family, having once lived just a block apart. Both families came from Beveren, so they may also have known each other in the old country. We do not know the details of how Elsie and Pete became got involved with each other, but my dad suspects my grandmother had to work to keep Grandpa "interested," since he was an attractive, well-traveled man of the world. "They used to like to get hamburgers at the Whiz-Bang Cafe," near the intersection of Front and Main Streets, when they were dating and first married, my dad remembered. "They used to like to play 'The Beer Barrel Polka.'"

Although Pete always treated Elsie's widowed mother with great care and respect, she still did not approve of the marriage of her only surviving child and feared they would abandon her. Pete even had to climb on top of the porch and sneak in through the second-floor window to see Elsie. When they were married on November 24, 1938, at St. Bavo Church, next-door to her home, Johanna Janssens refused to attend the ceremony. My grandparents lived with her at 520 West Eighth Street until her death in 1940.

Prior to getting married, Pete had returned to Mishawaka by at least 1936, the year the city directory lists him working at Major Brothers meatpacking plant as a "killer." He was soon laid off, and Achiel got him

My grandfather married my grandmother, Elsie Janssens, in 1938, around the time this photo was taken.

a job working with scrap metal at Ball Band. Grandpa worked for a while at Ball Band and then quit to go back to Major's, where he stayed until the early 1950s, when he began working for Schumacher Construction.

Pete's job at Major's provides some insightful anecdotes about the kind of person he was in those years. Wayne Linson was sixteen years old when he began working there, so Grandpa served as his mentor. Linson's mother was divorced, his father lived in Kokomo, and he had just quit school to work at Major's. "When I went to the slaughter-house, I acquired a father...His name was Pete De Kever," Linson said. "We just enjoyed each other...Pete was a different sort of a guy. He was kind of a loner till he got ahold of me, and I don't know why. But he could talk, he could laugh, he could have fun, he could tell you all kinds of stories. My God, the stories that man could tell you about his experiences and everything, and he'd had 'em all."

When Linson began, his boss told him to "'Stick with De Kever,'" and Grandpa took his new co-worker under his wing. Their main job working together was cleaning up the killing room, using big firehoses, at the end of a long day of slaughtering hogs or cattle. Pete told him, "'Believe me-- come with me; you'll make money.'" With their hard work, together they "had the place just shining," and Major's never had trouble passing the tough government health inspections.

Grandpa and Linson worked long days slaughtering animals and then another hour or two cleaning up. Killing began by 8 AM and went until 3 PM. Most of their work was with hogs, killing as many as 500 a day, but one day a week was cows. At the end of the day, he and Linson would sweep up the animal refuse and load it into carts before doing the heavy cleaning. Linson described Grandpa as one of the workers on the killing floor who could do any job there.

Linson shared many memories about the relationship he developed working with my grandfather. As Linson's time drew closer to being drafted into the army, Pete "tried to steer me right," Linson recalled, by saying, "'Don't volunteer for this, don't do that.'" Linson remembered, "When I went away to the army, I know he cried and so did I. He hugged me and he cried. I felt so bad. He said, 'You're going to be all right. Don't worry about this and that. When you get back, make sure you come and see me.' So when I came home on furlough, one of the first places that I went, I went to see him. He was so happy to see me...He was a guy I just loved as a young man." Pete also advised his young co-worker clear on money matters. When Linson went to buy a car, my grandfather advised him that buying a new car would be a wise investment that would grow in value because of the war. Linson bought a Ford for $800 and sold it for $1200 when he got home. "Pete steered me clear," he added.

While working at Major's may not have offered the excitement Grandpa experienced out West, it had its moments. Joe De Kever recalled, "I think he helped to save a co-worker on the killing floor when there was an ammonia leak."

Pete also befriended an African American co-worker named Otis Valentine. According to Linson, Valentine was often hurting himself on the job and toward the end of his career could not work much. "Pete did almost all his work, so he wouldn't get fired."

My father remembered that as a practical joke once, Grandpa brought home a pig's tail from the slaughterhouse to show my dad and Grandma. Wayne Linson recalled Grandpa putting a live mouse in someone's boot at Major's.

Although Peter slaughtered thousands of animals as part of his job, he refused to kill a rabbit for a friend, an action that offers insight into his values and gentle nature.

For the last twelve years of his life, Pete worked at Schumacher Construction on South Spring Street. For at least part of his time at Schumacher's, Grandpa was the yard manager, moving lumber and equipment, etc. He told Wayne Linson, "I do what I want. I just keep the place clean.'"

Several stories about Pete come from this period of his life. My dad recalled that when Grandpa worked at Schumacher's, he would go into work early in the morning and feed the squirrels around the company's office. He became such good friends with the squirrels they eventually ate out of his hand. Fred Gygi remembered Grandpa and Peter Schumacher were close friends, even though one was head of the company and the other was an employee. Gygi remembers Pete as a "witty" man with a good sense of humor.

Vignettes

In August 1994 my dad and I traveled to Iron Mountain and Norway, Michigan, and Little Chute, Wisconsin, to visit my grandmother's cousin, Harriet, and her husband, Norb. This trip gave us further insight about Grandpa. We learned that my grandparents took my great-grandmother De Kever to Norway and to Little Chute. My great-grandmother's cousins probably still lived in the Norway area; Joseph had come to America with his wife's uncle Louis Van Goethem in 1904. Several years later, after Norb and Harriet were married, they came to Mishawaka to visit my grandparents. Norb remembered Grandpa cleaned the engine of his car each week with a layer of degreaser, which helped the 1938 Chevy last until 1951.

My father has conveyed many other memories of my grandfather, which are further means by which Grandpa's memory lives on. He had

Pete De Kever plays with his son Joe, c. 1950.

My grandfather enjoyed fishing along the banks of the St. Joseph River. He is pictured with a catch in the back-yard of the family home at 523 West Eighth Street, c. 1960.

a Golden Echo harmonica, and my dad remembered Grandpa often playing "You Are My Sunshine." They also fished together along Northside Boulevard, west of the Logan Street Bridge, and when homes were built there, they went to Lincoln Park and along the opposite river bank. Pete kept a large garden in the small backyard of his home at 523 West Eighth. In the last years of his life, one of his sunflowers grew more than ten feet tall and was featured in the newspaper. Grandpa also donated money to the Salvation Army at Christmas because they helped his family get settled after they immigrated.

According to Joe De Kever, Grandpa was a private, complex man and had a side to him that my father rarely saw when growing up, such as playing jokes on people at work. A prop used in these jokes was a plaster egg which he would toss at people, who, for a moment, would expect to be covered with raw egg if their reaction was too slow. He must have done that often, for the egg is well chipped from many drops over the years.

Pete could also get emotional, yet kept it locked inside. For example, he might watch a sad television show and walk away with tears in his eyes.

Pete was also philosophical and, in his own way, religious. Wayne Linson explained, "He would go once and a while [to church] to satisfy his wife. He went on all the Easters and Christmas. No, he was not a big church man, but when she got after him, he would go." Although he did not regularly attend Mass, Grandpa tried to live by the basic teachings of the Church. When his mother lay dying in her home on Ninth Street, Pete drove to St. Bavo's to pick up Father Keller to give her last rites. Father brought the communion host in a small metal container, and Grandpa spoke afterward of how impressed he was that the body of the Lord had been in his car. My dad also remembered Grandpa had "a deep devotion to the Blessed Virgin," and "when he prayed, he always prayed three Hail Marys." In their backyard, Pete had a statue of Mary surrounded by a trellis which he would decorate with blue lights at Christmas. One of my grandfather's beliefs frequently mentioned by my dad was "'The dead won't hurt you; it's the living you have to worry about.'" He also said, "Life is for the living" and "'Some of the biggest hypocrites sit in the front row of church.'"

Pete was also loyal to his friends. An example of this involves his former boss at Major's, Raymond Plassaert, who was killed in a Christmas Eve car accident. In tribute to Plassaert, a member of the Eagles Club, Grandpa joined the club. In the years following, Pete went to the Eagles Club only once a year, such as on a Saturday night, to pay his membership dues and have some beers. He said he was going to "put a feather in the eagle" and stayed for several hours.

My father shared a miscellany of other memories. Grandpa had big hands and was strong and muscular, even though he was not tall. He and my dad would have contests to see who could squeeze the other's hand hardest, and my dad would always cry "uncle" first. Grandpa also had fun with his son by driving close to parked cars: "He had a tremendous sense of judgment of where his car was in relation to cars parked along the side." Although he was too old to serve in World War II, like many other men on the homefront, Pete was an air-raid warden in his neighborhood. One of his favorite recreations was reading **Official**

Detective Stories as he lay in bed on Saturday nights. He also took pleasure in getting up in the middle of the night and frying a steak. Pete also smoked a pipe, and, occasionally on summer evenings, he would sit on the small porch outside the kitchen and have a can of beer. Whenever anyone got a toothache, Pete's remedy was saying "okey-pokey" three times. While my grandfather was a world traveler in his youth, he traveled very little after returning to Mishawaka. According to my dad, "Probably the biggest trip that he took in the last 10-15 years of his life was to Nappanee."

In his final years, Grandpa suffered several heart attacks. Like many people of his generation, he ate a lot of eggs and other fried foods, but did not know that was unhealthy. He also kept his emotions to himself. These factors and the limitations of medicine at the time shortened his life.

Peter Ambrose De Kever died September 20, 1965, and is buried in Mishawaka's Fairview Cemetery.

Elsie and Pete De Kever had this photo taken at my parents' wedding in August 1965. Grandpa died less than a month later.

When we talk about visions of the dead, people tend to think of ghosts and other disembodied spirits, usually having malevolent intent. We need to reconsider this vision of the dead. Through memory and imagination, we can return the dead to life. In this way, people like my grandfather are still alive, their spirit animated once again in the mind's eye.

Part II

PLACES

CHAPTER 7

WEALTH OF KNOWLEDGE: ANDREW CARNEGIE AND THE MISHAWAKA PUBLIC LIBRARY

No individual is more closely associated with public libraries than Scottish-born steel baron Andrew Carnegie. In the late 1800s and early 1900s, Carnegie amassed a $360 million fortune, 90% of which he gave away to philanthropical causes to achieve what he referred to as "the improvement of mankind." As part of his Gospel of Wealth philosophy, Carnegie sought to help the poor and working class help themselves. Public libraries were an ideal way to achieve this goal.

Carnegie donated over $56 million to construct 2,509 library buildings in English-speaking countries. In the United States, 1,412 communities received $40 million of this sum for 1,679 public library buildings.

Indiana led the nation in the number of communities (155) and library buildings (164) involved in Carnegie's beneficence. Mishawaka's acquisition of the 147th Carnegie library building in Indiana reveals much about the process used to receive library buildings from Carnegie.

Like many communities Carnegie donated buildings to, Mishawaka already had a public library, established in 1907, but its 6,083 volumes were crammed into a 28'x30' room of the old City Hall on East First Street. In March 1909 John F. Nuner, superintendent of the Mishawaka schools, began correspondence with Andrew Carnegie, indicating, "As we are crowded now, we must look for more room in the near future and I wondered if you would not make us an offer of some kind for a building."

Carnegie Corporation archives show no further communication with Mishawaka until another Nuner letter in November 1913. Nuner noted the population growth of Mishawaka (5,560 in 1900 to 14,000 in 1913) and "great demand for a building here." Nuner informed Carnegie that "the City Council does not feel that it wants to take up the matter," and he hoped that Carnegie might work with the Board of Education instead.

Within a year the City Council's thinking had changed, and on December 2, 1914, it approved a resolution that pledged the city to annually provide a sum equal to 10% of the Carnegie gift, for maintenance and operating expenses.

Carnegie required this pledge from communities receiving library buildings. He believed that a library's long-term success depended on the community's financial support.

Carnegie boasted that he was actually getting towns to invest far more in their library than he was, for in just ten years, the community would contribute as much to its library as he had.

As was often the case with Carnegie libraries, the site for the new building was donated to the city. Local businessman Frederick G. Eberhart provided two lots on the 100 block of North Hill Street, across from then Mishawaka High School (today Mishawaka Furniture Company).

John Nuner sent Mishawaka's application materials to the Carnegie Corporation on December 23, 1914, and by January 6, James Bertram, Carnegie's personal secretary administering the library philanthropy, sent back his reply: "...if the city agrees by resolution of Council to maintain a Free Public Library, at a cost of Three Thousand Dollars ($3000) a year, and provides a suitable site for the bilding, Carnegie

Corporation of New York wil be glad to giv Thirty Thousand Dollars ($30,000) to erect a Free Public Library Bilding for Mishawaka, Indiana."

(Bertram and Carnegie both were believers in simplified spelling and practiced it in their correspondence.)

The $30,000 amount resulted from a formula that the Carnegie Corporation used to fund its building gifts: roughly $2 per resident. Mishawaka's 1915 population was nearly 15,000 and growing.

One criticism of the Carnegie library giving was that it inadequately accommodated future growth. Mishawaka's population doubled again by the end of the 1920s, and the city would soon have to expand its Carnegie building.

Nuner mentioned this concern in his January 11 reply to Bertram: "Every one in the city tonight was very much pleased at its announcement in the local papers...The only fear expressed is that the amount offered will not be sufficient to put us where we ought to be to start with and give us any margin for the future." Accordingly, Nuner asked for $35,000 instead, pointing to Mishawaka's rapid growth and the experiences of Goshen (Indiana's first Carnegie library recipient), Elkhart, and Kokomo. These towns felt that Mishawaka's estimates were conservative and desired larger buildings to accommodate their growth.

Bertram tersely denied Mishawaka's request, citing "the advance in knowledge of library planning" made it possible to build more economical buildings than when earlier Carnegie libraries were constructed.

In March 1915 a committee of fifteen local citizens was formed to oversee the library's design and construction. Nuner was chairman, and the rest of the committee included three school board members, the librarian, Mayor Ralph Gaylor, a councilman, Eberhart, and seven others.

By May 1915 Gary architect A.F. Wickes completed designs for the Mishawaka library, and Nuner sent them to Bertram for approval.

In 1911 Bertram and the Carnegie Corporation had translated their library experience into a publication, **Notes on the Erection of Library**

Buildings, which was sent to all communities receiving Carnegie funds. This led to some standardization of design, and Wickes' floor-plan was typical of many Carnegie libraries.

Bertram was not entirely satisfied with Wickes' original plans and reminded Nuner of Mishawaka's earlier concern about adequate funds: "In view of your previous attitude that $30,000 was insufficient to erect a bilding to meet the needs of Mishawaka, it would seem the greatest possible return should be gotten for the money expended in the bilding you do construct."

In his May 14 letter to Mishawaka, Bertram expressed concerns about the intended basement workroom being larger than needed and the "Social Room," which Bertram preferred to call a "lecture room," being too small. Bertram also wanted the basement ceiling lower and worried about whether the main floor windows would allow in adequate light. Nuner forwarded these concerns to Wickes, who was receptive to Bertram's ideas but defended the size of the lecture room and felt the light to be "ample."

Nuner further explained to Bertram that the committee was willing to make Bertram's changes, if he insisted, but decreasing the workroom "might encumber the staff ways a good deal and does not gain much desired room." Bertram was not satisfied, and the committee soon agreed to his changes, which included altering the windows and increasing by 50% the lecture room's capacity, to 200 persons. Nuner felt this still left "apparently plenty of room for work in the basement."

The long-distance dialogue continued during that summer, resolving Bertram's other concerns, such as the height of the main floor ceiling, the position of the staircase, the location of a partition, and the size of the librarian's office. Nuner and the Mishawaka committee were open to Bertram's ideas, but they did not change the design of the main staircase.

Construction bids for the library were received in August 1915, with the contract going to Ingwold Moe of Gary, with a price of $19,900. Construction began in early September 1915.

The Carnegie library had a frontage of 92' and a depth of 37', giving approximately 6800 square feet of space.

These photos show the main floor of the Carnegie library as it appeared after the WPA addition of the 1930s. At that time, the children's department was moved into the basement, where the auditorium had been.

The designs Bertram eventually approved succeeded at maximizing space and cost-effectiveness. The building had much open area, especially the 3400 square feet of the main level. The main floor included the adult reading area on the north end and the children's area on the south end. The circulation desk was centrally located and faced the Hill Street entrance. A barrel-vaulted ceiling and a massive wood-paneled fireplace, characteristic of the building's Jacobethan Revival style, were also prominent features of Wickes' design.

As for the exterior, Bertram's **Notes** was less specific, although it warned architects not to get carried away with elaborate designs that might interfere with an economical use of the interior.

Mishawaka's library differed from the common appearance of Carnegie-donated buildings, most of which used a Classical style to convey civic prestige. Wickes' more ornate design included Flemish-gabled end walls, a steeper slate tile roof, decorative ivory-colored terra cotta, leaded glass windows, parapet walls, and a large chimney protrud-

Mishawaka's Carnegie library was opened to the public on May 5, 1916.

This plaque was originally over the Hill Street entrance to the Carnegie library. It was moved to the north lobby of the new Mishawaka Public Library on Lincoln Way East in 1969.

ing to the south. Windows on the north facade of the main floor had stained-glass insets, including an open book, a scale, and an hourglass.

The Hill Street entrance was created for a striking impression. Four limestone columns surrounded the solid-oak door, with extensive terra cotta above the entrance. Over the door were the words "Pvblic Library," and above that a plaque reading, "An Idle Book Never Loses in Power. An Idle Man Does."

Most "Carnegie Classical" libraries featured a raised basement and prominent steps leading up to the main entrance. The Mishawaka building, though, featured an at-grade entrance.

The asymmetry of the Mishawaka library's west facade also made it unlike most Carnegie-donated buildings. The main entry vestibule was not centered, leaving the north end of the building eleven feet longer than the south end. Three large arched windows were north of the main entrance, with two to the south.

Today these features are still visible at the Carnegie library on North Hill Street. Only the plaque above the door has been removed and is in the north lobby of the Mishawaka-Penn-Harris Public Library on Lincoln Way East.

The Carnegie library was completed in late April 1916. The careful interchange between Mishawaka and Bertram hit one last snag in early May, when Bertram received a list of items bought for the building. The Carnegie Corporation intended its donation to be used only for items essential to the building's operation as a library. This sometimes caused confusion, though.

Bertram had to remind Nuner, "Trees and shrubs or pictures ar not part of a bilding. This Corporation promist a library bilding-- it did not promis an art gallery nor to plant a park."

Nuner responded that the error was unintentional and agreed to pay for the landscaping and pictures. But since Bertram had said items needed to finish the building should be paid out of the $30,000, Nuner passed along to the Carnegie Corporation some of the remaining costs for interior furnishings, which otherwise would have been paid with local money.

The public opening of the new building was Friday evening, May 5, 1916. In late April the **Mishawaka Enterprise** said, "No ceremonies will be held but the people are urged to visit the library and make a tour of inspection."

The old library in City Hall closed on May 1 to allow the staff to move books to Hill Street.

The move to the new facility led to an increase in the hours that the library was available to the public. In City Hall the library was open in the afternoons and evenings, but the Carnegie building would be open from 9 AM to 9 PM.

On opening day the **Enterprise** encouraged its readers: "Our citizens should take advantage of the invitation and show their appreciation of the royal gift by attending en masse." Mishawaka did turn out to open its new library building, which the **Enterprise** referred to as "Carnegie's Princely Gift." The paper noted, "The structure was crowded all the evening by hundreds of citizens, who were profuse in their expressions of approval and pleasure."

The **Enterprise** commented especially on the children's area: "In this room the little people will have every convenience and will enjoy a story hour every Saturday morning at 10 o'clock. The story teller will be provided by the Tri Kappa sorority." It is easy to imagine children gathered around the large fireplace at the south end of the main floor, listening with wide eyes as the nearby fire crackled.

Concluding its description of the opening, the **Enterprise** observed, "The library is something long desired and needed by Mishawaka, and our citizens should be profoundly grateful to the great philanthropist, Andrew Carnegie, for the generosity which has made its acquirement possible, and to Fred G. Eberhart for the donation of the site."

Mishawaka's Carnegie library was listed on the National Register of Historic Places in 1998.

While Mishawaka has not used the Carnegie building as a library since 1969, the Mishawaka-Penn-Harris Public Library on Lincoln Way East is still very much a Carnegie library. Andrew Carnegie and James Bertram wanted the donated building to be the catalyst for Mishawaka to support and value its public library. Carnegie would have asserted that a public library is as much a civic philosophy as it is a building. Carnegie's greatest gift to Mishawaka is the community's ongoing commitment to its public library.

CHAPTER 8

THE CURTAIN RISES AT THE TIVOLI, MISHAWAKA'S MOVIE PALACE

The most talked about issue in Mishawaka historic preservation in the 1990s was the restoration or demolition of the downtown's historic Tivoli Theater. While efforts to save the theater are well known, the origins and opening of the Tivoli in 1925 are easily forgotten. Thousands of Mishawakans today tell fondly their memories of the theater in the 1930s through 1960s, but those who remember the Tivoli's earliest days are all but gone now.

In an era when vaudeville and motion pictures were sweeping the country, hundreds of towns built theaters like the Tivoli. For many Americans the Roaring Twenties was a time of prosperity, youth-oriented culture, and mass entertainment.

In the mid-1920s, Mishawaka was Indiana's fastest growing city, a boom-town of over 20,000 people, doubling in population for the second time in the young century. Community boosters recognized that the downtown's two theaters each seated fewer than 1000 persons, and they wanted Mishawaka to be able to compete with the larger theaters of South Bend, accessible by interurban streetcar. The circumstances were ideal for a new theater to come to downtown Mishawaka.

In May 1924 Mishawaka was informed that a theater would be built on the 200 block of North Main Street. The Mishawaka Theater Corporation oversaw the project and consisted of local residents, including Mayor Duncan Campbell, and a Chicago investor. The corporation sold $110,000 worth of stock and took out a 99-year lease on the property.

After two houses belonging to Henry Buckels were removed from the site, construction of the theater began in the summer of 1924. E.P. Rupert, a Chicago theater architect, designed the building, and R. Levine and Company was the general contractor. In March 1925 the Mishawaka Theater Corporation announced the theater would be called "Tivoli," the name of Emperor Hadrian's villa in Ancient Rome. Mishawaka's new theater was completed in May 1925 at a cost of $275,000.

While the Tivoli Theater of today has been victimized by the elements and neglect, the Tivoli of 1925 was a state-of-the-art entertainment palace for the Princess City.

As opening night, May 21, 1925, neared, local newspapers published detailed descriptions of the theater, taking readers on an imaginary walking tour with Oscar J. Lambiotte, the theater manager, as guide. Lambiotte, a twenty-year veteran of the theater business, opened the Temple Theater (today Yorktowne Center at Main and Lincoln Way) in 1914. He left the Temple in 1920 to develop a chain of central Indiana theaters before returning to oversee the Tivoli, his "vision for a bigger, better theater for Mishawaka."

Along Main Street, the theater's marquee extended the width of the main entrance and over the width of the sidewalk. It was made of mostly bronze and art glass and had various colors of electric lights. The large arched window over the main entrance also was surrounded by lights. In the center of the window was a stained-glass inset with the letter **T**, and behind this window were wine-colored velvet drapes. Polychrome terra cotta eagles, crests, and garlands decorated the west facade of the building.

Adjoining the theater to the north, three storefronts and second-

The Tivoli Theater, shown here in 1937, was the city's premier performing arts venue after its opening in 1925.

floor office suites were constructed along Main Street. Five lanterns lined the rooftop of the building.

Entrance into the theater was through decorative glass doors into the lobby, where a sloped floor helped with crowd control. In the lobby the barrel-vaulted ceiling was indirectly lit, and iron staircases led up either side to the balcony. Extensive ornate plaster moldings added to the lobby's elegance.

In the lobby basement, parents could leave small children in a nursery during performances.

Art-glass doors led from the lobby into the main foyer, and the foyer and four aisles were covered in rich red Axminster carpet.

The three sections of the main floor had 950 blue leather seats. Mushroom vents brought heat and fresh air through giant pipes running under the concrete floor, keeping the building a constant 70 degrees.

Because the early Tivoli pictures were silent, a $22,500 Marr and

Colton Golden Throated Concert Organ provided musical accompaniment. The organ's pipes were behind large ornamental gratings rising up from either side of the orchestra pit, which also included a grand piano and a ten-piece orchestra for vaudeville. Miss Grace Goodwillie was the Tivoli's first organist.

The Tivoli stage measured 35'x28'. Six dressing rooms, three each on two levels, were above the south side of the stage, with four more dressing rooms below stage.

Built for an era without microphones, the Tivoli had ideal acoustics. Extending outward from the stage's proscenium arch, the flared ceiling was designed as an amplifying soundingboard and included three oil murals done by a Chicago artist, F. Myers.

Higher up and further back from the stage, red velvet draperies covered much of the walls, which were ivory, with gold, red, and blue tints.

The balcony, seating 450 and extending over nearly half of the lower level, was designed to give the upstairs audience the illusion that there was no audience on the lower level. The several rows of box seats were furnished with wicker chairs.

Directly above the balcony, a 24'-wide silver dome cast indirect light over the whole theater. A $3500 chandelier hung from the center of the dome.

Above the rear of the balcony was the projection booth, which included two projectors, a spotlight, and fireproof walls and door to protect against the hot lights and flammable celluloid film of that day.

The **South Bend News-Times** reporter was impressed by the new facility: "...the Tivoli, while not the largest theater in this section, is unsurpassed by any theater anywhere for intrinsic beauty, and it is wholeheartedly asserted that Mishawaka indeed has a theater of which it may be most justly proud."

As the Tivoli prepared for opening night, Lambiotte asserted his faith in the new building and its clientele: "I believe the Tivoli will be an asset to the community both socially and commercially, and I believe the citizenry of Mishawaka will demonstrate that our faith has not been misplaced. We want the Tivoli to stand as a concrete example of the very best in entertainment."

For a year Mishawaka had waited, eagerly watching the construction of the Tivoli, and, finally, by May 21, 1925, opening night had arrived.

Actually, the formal announcement of the opening of the theater came only at the last minute. Workers had been busy day and night trying to get the theater ready to open before the end of May. By mid-May all that remained was installing art glass in the foyer, and Lambiotte decided to open the theater right away.

Despite the short notice, the Tivoli drew capacity crowds for the two evening performances, at 7 PM and 9 PM. Between 2500 and 3000 attended opening night, and some waited in line for more than an hour. Admission for opening night was forty cents.

Before the first performance, ceremonies dedicated the theater. Mayor Duncan Campbell spoke briefly, stating that the theater marked an advance in Mishawaka's growth and cultural offerings.

The featured address of the evening came from Ralph Gaylor, president of the Mishawaka Chamber of Commerce. He acclaimed the

An audience of children gathers in front of the Tivoli, c. 1930s. Note the streetcar tracks on North Main Street.

theater builders' vision and belief in Mishawaka's future, a faith he hoped would be contagious. Gaylor said, "No one will claim that the Tivoli is the largest theater in the country, but there will be few who will not say that the Tivoli is one of the most beautiful, most modern, most convenient in this entire broad land of ours."

He also explained that the letters of **Tivoli**, when arranged in reverse order, spelled, "I love it." Gaylor noted, "Of course there is no **e** in **Tivoli**, but where there is real love a little thing like the absence of an **e** doesn't amount to much. And the people of Mishawaka should love this theater."

Mindful of his competition in South Bend, Oscar Lambiotte told the opening night audience, "Mishawaka has attained entertainment independence."

The Tivoli's opening bill was meant to preview the theater's policy of "furnishing the last word in theater entertainment for the residents

A full house of children enjoy a matinee at the Tivoli, c. 1930s. This may be the same group photographed in front of the theater. Note the children sitting on the railing of the orchestra pit.

of Mishawaka." It included three "high-class" vaudeville performances and a "photoplay." A full-page ad in the **Mishawaka Enterprise** claimed the Tivoli was "the Perfect Theater," with "a Show As Good As The Theater." The ad in the **South Bend Tribune** touted the Tivoli as "the finest theater it is possible to build" and promised to offer "the finest motion picture, stage and musical diversion obtainable in all the world."

After the dedicatory speeches, the entertainment began with a short motion picture, described by the **News-Times** as a "fantasy in colors, in which birds, fairies and flowers combined to make a thing of beauty." A comedy followed, and the feature was **The Dancers**, "a colorful story of New York and Tia Juana."

Opening the vaudeville portion of the evening was the Shannon Playtime Follies. The act consisted of two little girls, ages four and six-- "cute little tots," said the **Enterprise**-- performing tumbling and acrobatics with the help of their father. Their "perfectly executed...startling tricks" received great applause, according to the **News-Times**.

Crystal and Anderson came next and presented a "singing and talking act" that also met with a good response from the crowd.

The feature vaudeville act was Caulfield, Richie and Co., which included singing, dancing, orchestra music, and "pleasing lighting and scenic effects." Miss Richie danced with great skill and energy, despite having broken her foot on the way to Mishawaka, the **Enterprise** observed. Nonetheless, "the act went over with a bang."

To celebrate the successful opening night performances, a banquet followed at the Hotel Mishawaka (site of the post office today). The theater corporation invited about a hundred guests, including Tivoli stockholders, city officials, clergy, and other community leaders.

Friday and Saturday repeated the opening night performances, and on Sunday a special bill included new vaudeville acts and motion pictures. Performances ran continuously from 1:15 PM through 11 PM, with vaudeville at 3 PM, 6:45 PM, and 9 PM. The movies were **For Sale** and **French Pastry**, a comedy. The vaudeville included Harry Weber's Springtime Review Novelty Dancers.

Beginning Monday and continuing through Wednesday with matinees on the following Saturday and Sunday, Tom Mix, the most famous cowboy film star of the 1920s, was featured in **Teeth**, with "Tony the Horse and Duke the Dog." The film was advertised as "A big drama of the west-- The kind you love to see Tom Mix in."

With the Tivoli's opening week coming to a close, the downtown Mishawaka institution had been successfully established. In the decades to come, thousands of Mishawakans of all ages would make the Tivoli Theater an important part of their lives.

By the late 1960s, though, changes in the economics of the entertainment industry closed the Tivoli as a movie and live performance theater for the general public.

The Tivoli Theater was listed on the National Register of Historic Places in 1998.

Today, more than 75 years after its opening night, the empty, dark Tivoli Theater awaits the excited energy of an audience and performers, eager for the curtain to be raised again.

CHAPTER 9

BEYOND THE LEGEND: THE WILLARD ALDRICH HOUSE AND LIFE ON THE NORTH SIDE IN THE 1920S

Gambler, atheist, and horse thief, are a few terms that have been used to describe Mishawaka's Willard Aldrich, who died of tuberculosis in 1882. While his life as a horse trader (among other things) attracted some attention, it was moreso Aldrich's plans for his burial that created the most eccentric legend in Mishawaka history.

Many have heard of the special casket Aldrich had made that would allow him to sit upright for eternity. His grave in Mishawaka's City Cemetery also included a 5'x7' vault with walls covered with pictures of cowboys and Indians fighting, favorite horses, and beautiful women. Likewise, Aldrich added a table with a deck of playing cards, whisky bottle, pipe and tobacco, as well as a saddle, boots, and shotgun intended for when Satan came calling.

Willard Aldrich's Egyptian-like tomb has intrigued local citizens for over a century and remains the most popular stop on tours of City Cemetery. For lifelong Mishawaka resident Charles Kuhn, the Aldrich

Charles Kuhn, shown here in 1998, was born in the Willard Aldrich house in 1915.

legend was more than just a grave stocked for the afterlife.

Kuhn was born in the Willard Aldrich house on January 6, 1915. Originally, the Aldrich home stood atop a high, tree-shrouded hill, long since leveled, in the middle of the block south of Battell and east of Main, near the old Battell School. Kuhn's grandfather, John Kuhn, told Charles "that he bought the house from Aldrich's mother...She lived there after he died, and my granddad bought-- from what I understand-- half of the house, and the other half stayed there." Mrs. Aldrich died in 1892. John Kuhn moved the house to 115 West Battell, where it stands today.

Charles was not sure if his grandfather knew Willard Aldrich, who died when John Kuhn was 18. Kuhn supposed, "He must 'a' had an eye on that house because, otherwise...well, he'd probably build another one, but he must've liked it just the way it was built."

According to Charles Kuhn, his grandfather put the house on 1 3/4 lots, setting it on a foundation of huge rocks, rather than on cement. A

Michigan-style basement, 12'-15' across, extended under part of the house, with a crawl space under the rest. John Kuhn made wine in the basement, and Charles recalled seeing the wine kegs when he was growing up during Prohibition.

John Kuhn owned four houses in the Battell-Lawrence neighborhood. Charles' parents were living with his grandparents when he was born in Aldrich's house. Around 1916-17, Charles' family moved to West Marion Street, but he frequently visited his grandparents' nearby home. His memories highlight what life was like in that northside neighborhood 80 years ago.

Kuhn remembered well details of the Aldrich house. A porch wrapped around the front and side of the home. The downstairs had 10' ceilings, a parlor, living room, dining room, kitchen, walk-in closet, and, in later years, a bathroom. A hallway went alongside the parlor and living room to the stairway, which was by the front door. He recalled, "It had a big banister. We used to slide down that."

John Kuhn moved half of the Aldrich home to 115 West Battell Street, where Charles Kuhn had many childhood memories.

The upstairs included eight-foot ceilings, a wide hall, large landing, two walk-in closets, and four bedrooms. Kuhn vividly remembered the types of windows in three of the four upstairs bedrooms: "The windows in the upstairs was right down to the floor, bottom clear to the floor. The sill of the windows at the bottom of the room."

The Kuhns also had a summer kitchen on the back of the house. Entry to the basement was from the summer kitchen through two large doors in the floor. Nearby were two coal bins-- soft coal for cooking and hard coal for heating the living room. John Kuhn also had a walk-in chicken coop in the back and large gardens on the side and rear of the house.

Charles Kuhn learned about Aldrich when visiting his grandparents, including one story about Aldrich's relations with the police: "I was told that whenever he went out and stole a horse and the law got after him, he would take and lay down on the floor with his mother, looking out these windows to see when the law was coming to get him." Kuhn remembered, as a boy, laying on the floor upstairs and looking

Willard Aldrich is buried under this slab in the Mishawaka City Cemetery.

through those same windows toward Battell School or downtown.

Kuhn was told that when the police were coming, Aldrich and his mother "would take and go down in the lower floor and pull the rug back...It was in the parlor that the trap door was at." Aldrich would hide in the crawl space, "and she'd pull the rug back over it, and the law would leave, and she'd go back upstairs and see if they were leaving or sticking around. And when she thought they'd left, she'd come down, let him back out." Charles Kuhn recalled that his uncle later used that trap door to hide whisky during Prohibition.

In addition to the ties to Willard Aldrich, Kuhn remembered the West Battell neighborhood was not immune to a dark side of the 1920s: the Ku Klux Klan.

Kuhn told of one experience he had with the Klan. When he was around ten or twelve, the city was putting in a new sewer line in front of his grandparents' house, creating a huge mound of dirt. One night, "all of a sudden, commotion's out in the front. And here the Ku Klux Klan had set up a cross [on the mound] and set it on fire."

Kuhn believed this may have been done to intimidate either the Catholics, immigrants, African Americans, or the woman allegedly involved in prostitution, who all lived on that block. All of these people, especially Catholics, were targets of the Indiana KKK when it was at the height of its power in the 1920s. While census records do not list religious affiliation, they do show that in the 1920s the 100 block of West Battell included two African Americans and a family with three Russian immigrants.

Kuhn speculated about whom the Klan was targeting. The burning cross was in front of the line separating his grandparents' house from the house to the west, where the woman in prostitution lived. He recalled, "It was the mother, the one they were targeting. As far as I understood...she was controlling...young gals. My granddad was Catholic, and she was a prostitute."

Regardless of the target, the cross-burning got the attention of the whole block. Kuhn said, "They all come out of the houses. Sure, they was all out on the street. It was something. The Klan was awful powerful back then around here."

Charles Kuhn remembered fondly two African Americans, Alonzo and Clara Pompey, who lived across the street from John Kuhn: "They were nice people because they used to come over to our grandparents' all the time. [Alonzo]'d take and play with us. I've never been against coloreds in my life because I was raised that way...We didn't have no trouble, but the Ku Klux Klan wanted to stir stuff up."

The Aldrich house passed out of the Kuhn family in the 1940s, but not out of the memory of Charles Kuhn. His recollections of the Aldrich house and growing up in the West Battell neighborhood provide a valuable personal link to the Aldrich story and the lifestyles and social tensions experienced in Mishawaka in the 1920s.

CHAPTER 10

SECOND CHANCES: THE WPA AND THE MISHAWAKA RESERVOIR CARETAKER'S RESIDENCE

For decades Americans have been touched by the lasting effects of the Great Depression. Images of long lines of unemployed and stories of sacrifices, sharing, and perseverance all endure in the nation's memory. So, too, do more tangible remnants of that era in the form of construction projects completed by public works programs, such as the Works Progress Administration.

While Franklin D. Roosevelt's WPA was often criticized as a wasteful, make-work program for the unemployed, it provided some of the New Deal's most enduring contributions to modern American life. Established by Congress in 1935, the WPA followed earlier governmental programs, such as the Federal Emergency Relief Administration, which provided relief money to the unemployed in 1933; the Public Works Administration, which did large-scale construction projects, such as dams; and the Civilian Conservation Corps, which emphasized work in state and national parks and forests.

Under the direction of Harry Hopkins, the WPA was an urban-oriented response to the needs created by the Depression, most notably getting able-bodied people back to work and off the direct-relief rolls. Early New Deal programs such as FERA had given direct payments to the unemployed, but Hopkins realized that money alone could not meet the most important needs of the unemployed: "Only a work program can answer...all aspects of the unemployment problem. Only a job can answer the problem of a jobless man; only a wage will increase purchasing power...only through work can these people make their contribution to our national well-being."

The WPA was a federal, state, and local partnership. Local governments sponsored projects and provided land, tools, and building materials. With coordination from district and state WPA offices, federal funds paid labor expenses. Because local money was often hard to come by, materials were often donated, reclaimed from demolished buildings, or gathered from the natural environment.

Hard hit by the Depression's toll on its heavy industry, Indiana was a major recipient of WPA assistance. Hoosier WPA workers constructed armories, parks, wading pools, athletic fields, gymnasiums, streets, and airports, and taught arts and crafts classes and reorganized county records.

As much as any community, Mishawaka suffered from the effects of the Depression on its industry and benefited from the WPA. In 1938 the WPA employed 500 workers in Mishawaka and nearly 5000 in St. Joseph County. WPA workers in Mishawaka rebound books, remodeled and expanded the Carnegie Library, constructed new sewer lines and municipal buildings, and repaired and improved streets throughout the city. The most lasting WPA landmarks in the Princess City are the elaborate fieldstone rock gardens of Battell Park, the rock walls lining the St. Joseph River from the Eberhart-Petro Golf Course to Logan Street, the development of Kamm Island, Monkey Island, and Central Park, and the construction of Mishawaka High School's football stadium.

One of the most distinctive and significant elements of the WPA's work in the city was the Mishawaka Reservoir caretaker's residence on Ireland Trail. This house reveals a chapter of the WPA's work in Mishawaka, a part of the state and national history of the WPA, and efforts today to preserve the WPA's legacy.

The caretaker's residence, shown here in 1994, was completed in 1938.

A Reservoir in the Hills

The story of the Mishawaka Reservoir caretaker's residence begins with the tremendous population increase that Mishawaka experienced in the 1920s. From 1922 to 1927, water customers increased in Mishawaka from 3,400 to 5,250, and the water system grew from 34.4 miles to 58.3 miles. Water consumption rose by over 1.2 million gallons per year in the 1920s, and the water department expected this rate of increase to continue.

To cope with this growth and increasing water demand, Austin R. Klein, general superintendent of the Mishawaka Water and Electric Department, proposed to the mayor and Board of Public Works in June 1928 that the city improve its water system by constructing an additional high-service pump and a reservoir in the hills south of town. He wrote, "...a storage reservoir would accomplish the same result as [a] second transmission main and...would improve the operation of the pumping equipment [and] would also provide additional capacity for peak loads."

The city proceeded to purchase land south of Dragoon Trail and east of Ireland Trail, a mile and a half south of downtown. The 8.1 acre tract was bought from Amedio C. Nardi in September 1928. The land and construction were paid for by a $100,000 bond issue.

Construction began in the spring of 1929, and the reservoir went into operation late that year. Measuring 143 square feet and 21 feet deep, it was built of reinforced concrete covered with a concrete lid, under 18 inches of topsoil. The reservoir was built at an elevation 160' higher than the river, which contributed to its value for maintaining pressure in the city's water system. The reservoir had a capacity of 3 million gallons and gave static pressure of 60-70 pounds throughout the system. Two 20" cast-iron mains connected the reservoir to the city's main water lines.

The completion of the reservoir in the fall of 1929 coincided with the stock market crash and the beginning of the Great Depression. By 1933 Franklin Roosevelt's New Deal was underway, and by 1935 the WPA was carrying out public works construction projects across the country.

Water supply projects were common during the New Deal. Many communities were able to improve their water systems with the aid of federal programs like the WPA. From 1933 to 1939, $112 million was spent by various federal agencies to aid municipal water projects.

Mishawaka received its share of help from the federal government to upgrade and expand the water system of the growing city. Among its Mishawaka projects, the WPA worked on sewers, built a new dual main feeder line for the reservoir, and constructed a storage building for the water department.

A Work in Progress

Problems at the city reservoir caused Mishawaka and the Works Progress Administration to collaborate on yet another project: the construction of a caretaker's residence.

On November 1, 1937, Austin Klein wrote W.H. Jordan, the district director of the WPA in South Bend: "There is no police protection and the only inspections [of the reservoir] are made twice weekly by employees of the Water Department." Klein also submitted a proposal application that stated whenever the gates of the reservoir were found "disturbed or opened," the city had been compelled to drain the reservoir to be sure no contamination of the water supply had occurred. Klein noted each draining incident cost the city "several hundred dollars."

To solve this problem, Klein wrote that the Board of Public Works, after reviewing "several plans," chose the option of a residence, located next to the reservoir itself, and "occupied by a responsible party, having authority as caretaker" as "the most reliable protection." Because the WPA would not fund anything but construction owned by a government and serving a public function, the application specified, "This project is not proposed for purpose of gathering revenue but to house a custodian for protective measures." The WPA generally did not construct single-family dwellings, so the city was careful to note that this house would be used in a manner consistent with other WPA projects.

Jordan, in support of this proposal, submitted a November 4, 1937, letter to V.J. Cox, assistant director of the Division of Operations for the WPA in Indianapolis. Jordan hoped for a quick approval "so operations could be started by the middle of December." He also noted that Mishawaka had cooperated "one hundred percent" with the WPA and felt it would be "to our advantage to cooperate with them in this instance."

Klein's proposal included this description of the project:

> *Excavations; foundations; construction of superstructure complete; building chimney and fireplace; installation of electrical, heating, water and plumbing facilities; building septic tank; leveling and landscaping adjacent grounds...*

These plans also included cost estimates for labor, materials, and equipment. Unskilled labor was predicted to cost $1,440, "intermediate" labor was $1,235, and skilled labor took most of the remaining labor costs at $2,890. One superintendent position was also budgeted for $560, which brought total labor estimates to $6,125. The proposal listed all of the labor costs as coming from federal funds; whereas, all but $332 of the materials and equipment expenses would be paid for by the local sponsor, the Mishawaka Water and Electric Department. Total estimated costs of materials and equipment for the project were $4,109. Labor, materials, and equipment for the entire project totaled $10,234, no small sum for a modest residence in 1937.

The application further analyzed the labor element of the project. Six unskilled laborers were planned for the project, working 120 hours per month each for the four-month project at $60 per month. Five "laborers general" were planned at 120 hours per month for 19 man-months, earning $65 per month.

The skilled labor planned for the caretaker's residence was described in more detail. Five carpenters, six bricklayers, one cement finisher, one sheet-metal worker, two painters, one plumber, one electrician, one timekeeper, and the superintendent completed the labor force. The skilled laborers worked varying hours per month: carpenters 85, bricklayers 68, cement finisher 70.5, sheet-metal worker 85, painters 96.5, plumber 75, and electrician 85. The expected working period was 120 hours per month, which meant these workers did not have 40-hour weeks. WPA projects were not intended to be either full-time or long-term employment. Skilled laborers earned $85 per month, and the superintendent was paid $140 per month. The November 1937 proposal anticipated 30 workers for the project.

The remainder of the application detailed materials and equipment costs. As the local sponsor, the city had to pick up the tab for a 1 1/2-ton truck, at a rate of $1.30 per hour for 360 hours, for a total of $468. Beyond this, federal funds only picked up $330 for cement and $2 for first-aid supplies. The application listed materials-related expenses:

110 barrels of Portland cement	$330
face brick	$300
common brick	$288
6 cubic yards of field stone	$ 36
2200 1-lb iron reinforcing rods	$ 88
plumbing material	$410
electric pump	$110
hot air furnace	$106

electric wiring and fixtures	$160
25 gallons of paint	$ 75
sheet metal material	$ 75
200 feet of 6" tile	$ 20
200 feet of 4" drain tile	$ 10
Dimension lumber	$482.80
interior trim and millwork	$984
two tons of plaster	$ 40
3125 square feet of sheet rock lath	$125

These items, supplied by the local project sponsor, totaled $3309. The final page of the proposal application gave other evidence about the scope of the project:

500 cubic yards of excavation	$500
70 cubic yards of concrete for the foundation and floors	$1400
25 cubic yards of concrete reinforced slab floors and coping	$875
putting exterior brick in place	$800
laying common brick	$960
fireplace and chimney	$400
a septic tank	$200
painting and decorating	$300
leveling and landscaping	$215

Mayor Edward C. Went signed the application, certifying that funds pledged by the local sponsor would be available if the application were approved and the federal government picked up the labor costs.

Work on the house did not start in December, as Jordan had hoped. In February 1938, though, the **South Bend Tribune** reported that the project was to begin "as soon as weather will permit," and was expected to employ 30 men for 60 working days.

Construction of the caretaker's residence began on March 2, 1938.

A Delay and a Letter to Washington

Problems developed with the project by April 1938. A project proposal supplement, dated April 29, was sent to W.H. Jordan, who, in turn, sent a letter on May 18 to John R. Curry, Director of WPA Operations, in Indianapolis. This letter and the supplement proposal asked for $2,085 in additional funds. Jordan explained the status of the project: "The work on the original project is moving along rather rapidly and these additional funds will be necessary to satisfactorily complete the structure." He added a more insistent closing to the letter:

> *If these additional funds are not approved prior to the exhaustion of funds on the original project, it would be necessary to suspend operations and this would leave the structure in a state where rain or vandalism would destroy a considerable amount of the work already completed.*

Jordan's letter and supplementary funds proposal were accompanied by a letter from Austin Klein to John K. Jennings, Indiana's WPA administrator. Klein defended the cost of labor for this supplementary proposal: "yet in consideration of the type of construction, this figure is believed reasonable." Klein was aware that Mishawaka would only contribute 2% of the supplement, but noted that Mishawaka was funding 31% of the total project, which he hoped would weigh in the city's favor. He reminded Jennings of the need for this project, that the city would have been unable to fund it on its own without the WPA, and noted, "This department has always endeavored to provide the Works Progress Administration with projects of a constructive and permanent value, and our full cooperation will be extended this proposal."

Klein and Jordan's efforts succeeded in earning support from Indianapolis. On May 30 Jennings sent a letter of request for the funds to G.E. Traxtor, Acting Director of the Project Control Division of the WPA, in Washington, DC.

What caused this over-run? Jennings' letter to Traxtor vaguely explained, "Funds on the original project are being expended at a faster rate than was anticipated at the time the subject application was submitted." The project proposal supplement form told a little more: "Original unit estimates were too low and trouble was experienced that was not anticipated when the original project was prepared." No details were given for what that "trouble" was, though.

The rest of the application provided details on what additional labor and materials were asked for to finish the house. Nearly all of the $2,085 in extra costs went for labor. Federal funds were requested for $2,023.33 in labor expenses and only $1.67 in material-related costs. The city would pick up the remaining $60 for materials and supplies. Line 19 of the application said 15 working days were still needed for completion, yet page 3 suggests a full month of work when it lists the number of workers and the man-months remaining. Only 26 men were working on the project: five unskilled laborers, eight general laborers, four plasterers, one bricklayer, one electrician, one plumber, five painters, and the superintendent.

In late May 1938, Jennings received word from Traxtor that the project supplement "was signed by the President on May 23 and currently awaits clearance by the Comptroller General."

The supplementary funds application shows the final cost of the project was $12,319, with $8,482 from the WPA (69%) and $3,837 from the city (31%). Of the total pricetag, $8,148 went for labor and $4,171 was for materials, supplies, and equipment.

A Plaque for the Finished Project

A distinguishing feature of the Mishawaka Reservoir caretaker's residence is a limestone plaque embedded in the outside wall. This plaque, which denotes the house's construction by the WPA, also has a story behind it, documented in the National Archives' WPA files.

On April 30, 1938, W.H. Jordan at the district office in South Bend sent a letter to John Curry in Indianapolis. This correspondence offers background on the marker:

> *On April 7 this office placed an order for corner stones that are needed for permanent marking of WPA projects in the First District. These stones are for...construction of a caretaker's resi-*

This plaque embedded on the side of the caretaker's residence was made by WPA stonecutters in Bedford, Indiana.

dence at the site of the Mishawaka water reservoir, the inscription to read "Built by Federal Works Progress Administration, 1937-1938"; also one for...water distribution system in the Town of Lakeville, the inscription to be "Built by Federal Works Progress Administration, 1937-1938."

A representative of this office, Mr. William L. Lockhen, will be in the vicinity of Bedford on Tuesday, May 3 and will want to obtain these stones if they are finished, so that he can bring them to the district when he returns, thereby saving transportation costs to this location. I will appreciate your efforts to inform the project immediately to release these markers to Mr. Lockhen.

Indiana WPA historian Glory June Greiff notes that Bedford was a likely source for the carved cornerstone. As construction of buildings using limestone slowed greatly during the Depression, most of Lawrence County's stonecutters were unemployed or underemployed and found work through the WPA. Parks in Bedford today have much detailed stonework done by these cutters under the WPA's auspices. The stone marker and the caretaker's residence are linked, both being efforts to help unemployed Hoosiers in two parts of the state in 1938.

The National Archives has no further documentation related to the house after the flurry of letters and documents in the spring of 1938 pertaining to the supplement.

On February 23, 1939, the **Mishawaka Enterprise** reported that the house had been finished in December, giving no explanation for the extended delay, when in the spring it seemed like only a month was needed for completion.

With the help of the Works Progress Administration, Mishawaka now had a caretaker's house to protect the reservoir. In a little over a year, the project had been conceived, approved, and completed. From here on, it would not be the WPA shaping the history of the house, but rather its inhabitants, who called it a home.

A Walk Through the Caretaker's Residence

The WPA-built house mimicked the appearance of an English cottage. Built in a rectangular plan, it consisted of three floors: an entry-level main floor, a walk-in attic extending the full length and width of the house, and a full basement with a rear outside entrance.

The main floor included a living room, dining room, kitchen, bathroom, and two bedrooms, altogether totaling less than a thousand square feet.

The exterior of the home was brown-orange Chicago common brick. The house had ten distinctive narrow windows, and all the windows were steel casements and had concrete lintels. Decorative brick soldier courses ran in a continuous line above the first-floor windows and above the foundation. Just behind the ridgeline of the side-gabled roof rose the chimney stack, composed of fieldstone with raised mortar.

In front of the house, running from the front door to the south was a raised-mortar fieldstone wall enclosing a flagstone patio-porch. A trellis porch roof surrounded the front door.

The solid construction done by the WPA was evident in the house. The entire exterior of the house was 9"-thick load-bearing brick walls. The first floor was a 7"-thick slab of poured concrete, supported by a skeleton of iron reinforcing bars. The basement had 9"-thick walls.

The caretaker's residence and the reservoir were on a plateau rising twenty feet above Ireland Trail. With the reservoir immediately north of the house, it was a good location for a watchman's residence. Steep hills to the north, west, and east would have made any trespasser approach the reservoir by going past the caretaker's residence first. The only vehicle entrance onto the property went alongside the house.

The labors of the WPA created a solid, attractive, yet simple house by the end of 1938. Situated in the quiet Mishawaka Hills, the caretaker's residence would have been an attractive home for its first residents in early 1939.

The Project Becomes a Home

The **Mishawaka Enterprise** of February 23, 1939, reported that the Board of Public Works and William D. Buckles had signed a lease for him to occupy the house as its first resident. In return for residency, Buckles would provide "specified watchman and caretaker service."

Buckles and his wife Allie had left the house by 1943, when Mrs. Buckles died after a lengthy illness.

Floyd Swartzlander, his wife Violet, and their three young children moved into the home in February 1944. Swartzlander had worked as a lineman for the electric department since June 1942. The Swartzlander family lived in the caretaker's residence for less than a year and left under tragic circumstances.

On October 13, 1944, Floyd Swartzlander and another lineman were working atop a 35-foot pole repairing a transformer in the alley behind the Tivoli Theater. High-tension wires crossed and exploded in a fireball, forcing Swartzlander and his partner to drop quickly down a rope with their clothing on fire.

Swartzlander suffered third-degree burns head to foot and succumbed to his injuries on October 28. Within weeks after Swartzlander's death, his wife and children left the caretaker's residence and returned to Bremen.

The city did not leave the caretaker's residence empty for long before its next tenants, Dwight and Mabel Snyder, took residence in late 1944 or early 1945. The Snyders were married in Mishawaka in 1940 and were both in their early forties when they moved into the house.

Dwight Snyder, Jr., and his wife Virginia have provided extensive information about the house, its residents, and the surrounding reservoir property during the 47 years that their family was associated with the home.

Snyder explained that his father, also a lineman for the electric department, and step-mother were offered the house by Austin Klein for $15 rent per month if Dwight, Sr. would take on the duties of caretaker/watchman for the reservoir.

An Evolving House and Grounds

Dwight and Virginia Snyder recalled a variety of details about the house and the reservoir site.

Mr. Snyder remembered when the furnace was converted from coal to oil after the war. Because the oil furnace required forced-air heating, as opposed to coal's gravity heating, air hammers were used to create additional ducts in the concrete slab. Snyder also recalled coal was poured down a chute under the bay window into a coal bin in the basement.

Dwight Snyder also explained that the water supply for the house came directly from the reservoir, not from a well.

Above many of the first-floor windows were awnings with forest-green and white stripes. Dwight, Sr. made wood storm windows to hang over the casement windows installed by the WPA.

Dwight, Jr. also remembered being told that some of the brick used in the caretaker's residence came from a demolished water tower near the old City Hall on First Street. While none of the documents from the National Archives confirms this, it would be consistent with the WPA's frequent use of reclaimed materials.

Around the exterior of the house, Dwight and Mabel Snyder maintained the grounds with a "stately appearance," according to their son and daughter-in-law. Mabel, especially, loved flowers and gardening. She planted raspberry bushes, tiger lilies, and other plants, and had pots and planters around the home. A garden behind the house provided Mabel with food for cooking and canning, and she used a small room in the basement to store canned foods and preserves. She also grew plants there with fluorescent lighting.

Daily Life at the House

Dwight and Virginia Snyder described Mabel as "an immaculate housekeeper and good cook" before her health began to fail in the 1980s. Inside the house they recalled English cottages and figurines adorning the fireplace mantel. Boston ferns and other plants thrived in the light streaming through the bay window. Mabel enjoyed sewing and crochet, and used one bedroom as a sewing room. Her handiwork decorated the house as curtains, bedspreads, chaircovers, and other embroidery. She also made many of her own clothes.

The Snyders always had dogs when they lived at the caretaker's residence, as well as horses until Dwight, Sr. died in 1969.

Dwight Snyder recalled that his parents and their friends would ride horses on the reservoir property and through the surrounding countryside, which, in the 1940s and 1950s, would have been quieter and more rural than in later years. They rode as far as Kern Road and Elm Road, and throughout the Mishawaka Hills near the reservoir.

Dwight and Mabel Snyder had their own dogs, but also cared for the large German shepherds the city kept inside the reservoir fence as an added defense against intruders.

Dwight, Jr. recounted that whenever the reservoir guard dogs barked at night, his father would grab a flashlight and investigate the source of the disturbance. Rarely, though, was there ever any real threat to the reservoir when the dogs barked. If anyone was on the property, most likely they were just harmless trespassers. The Snyders would occasionally find lovers hiding in the secluded parts of the property, and Dwight, Sr. or, in later years, Mabel, would use a powerful flashlight to seek out the amorous intruders.

The caretaker's residence also provided relief from hot summer weather. Virginia Snyder remembered that she and her husband would take ice cream up to Mabel in her later years. Even on hot days, the thick brick and cement of the house kept it cool inside.

An Era Draws to a Close

Mabel Snyder lived alone in the caretaker's residence from her husband's death in 1969 until January 1990, when she was moved into a nursing home. This ended half a century of habitation of the house, 47 years of which she had lived there. Understandably, utilities workers and others who frequented the property had taken to calling it "Mabel's House."

Because of Mabel's age and the length of the Snyders' service, the city allowed her to live there as long as she wanted, continuing as a faithful caretaker for the reservoir. City officials, though, had decided that no one else would live there after her. In Mabel's later years, the house had fallen into disrepair, with her not being able to care for it well and the city assuming an attitude of benign neglect. The cost of repairs and the perceived lack of need for the house led the city to board it up, awaiting eventual demolition.

Mabel Snyder died in January 1994 at age 92. Her departure from the caretaker's residence ended one era of the house's history. It also began to raise fears that the deteriorating, empty house may have outlived its usefulness and seen its last resident.

Saving an Endangered Landmark

In late 1992 the Mishawaka Historic Review Board expressed concern about the future of the abandoned WPA-built house. For the next three years, the caretaker's residence was the subject of further inquiry by the Review Board. Although the house was outside the city limits and the Review Board's legal jurisdiction, the group could make recommendations to city officials and serve as an advocate for the house's preservation.

The St. Joseph County Historic Preservation Commission also was aware of the house and conducted some preliminary negotiations with the City of Mishawaka to ensure that the residence would not be demolished. When the utilities department seemed uncooperative, the Historic Preservation Commission even considered a unilateral declaration of the house as a county historic landmark, to prevent its demolition.

In 1993 and early 1994, various adaptive reuses for the house were considered, and several potential buyers looked at the home. None of these possibilities developed beyond the inquiry stage.

Because of pressure from historic preservation groups, Mayor Robert Beutter and city officials were reluctant to simply tear the house down. Instead, the city chose to sell the house with the stipulation that the buyer would have to move it off the reservoir property. The house was put up for public auction, and the only bid received was for $11 from the Beiger Heritage Corporation, a Mishawaka historic preservation group.

Once Beiger Heritage acquired the building, it considered various

In the summer of 1995, the caretaker's residence was removed from the city reservoir property.

On August 1, 1995, the house traveled the short distance down Ireland Trail to a new location on Chandler Boulevard.

options for where the house would finally go. The group looked at placing the house in Lincoln Park or Battell Park or selling to a private buyer who would move it east to a lot on Dragoon Trail. The city had no interest in allowing the caretaker's residence on park property, and the private buyer lost interest in the project.

Beiger Heritage chose its only remaining option: moving the house to Chandler Boulevard, a third of a mile south of the reservoir. The home would then be renovated and sold as a private residence with restrictive covenants to protect the historic facade of the building.

Rapid progress was made on the extensive planning needed to complete the project. A wooded lot was purchased in February 1995, and by April a basement was constructed, replicating the thickness of the original basement's walls.

The process of moving the house began in mid-June. Lykowski Construction of South Bend knocked holes in the thick basement walls so they could place a cradle of iron support beams underneath the house, in preparation for lifting it. Lykowski's workers noted that the cement in the basement of the caretaker's residence was the hardest material they had ever worked with. Smashing holes in the basement actually damaged their jackhammers.

By early July the 200-ton house was lifted above the foundation, and by July 20 the house was a mobile home, sitting atop several sets of hydraulic dollies, each capable of bearing 75 tons. After delays due to weather and the need to move electric lines, the caretaker's residence was finally moved to Chandler Boulevard on August 1, 1995. Restoration continued through the following months, in preparation for selling the house to a private buyer.

The Mishawaka Reservoir caretaker's residence was listed on the National Register of Historic Places in 1998.

The Caretaker's Residence Today

More than 60 years after its construction, the Mishawaka Reservoir

Its restoration complete, the Mishawaka Reservoir Caretaker's Residence is listed on the National Register of Historic Places.

caretaker's residence links modern Mishawaka with the Great Depression and Works Progress Administration.

Historically and architecturally, the house is a rarity. WPA historian Glory June Greiff refers to the caretaker's residence as "a significant and rare example of WPA construction." She observes that the WPA rarely built single-family homes, and the Mishawaka Reservoir caretaker's residence is the only such house built on municipal land in Indiana. The few other WPA-built custodial cottages in Indiana were on state-owned land, and the only extant examples of these buildings have been significantly altered. Greiff feels the Mishawaka house "stands alone as a remarkably intact example of WPA workmanship applied to domestic architecture."

The significance of the Mishawaka Reservoir caretaker's residence transcends its architectural uniqueness. In one of history's ironies, the story of this house parallels that of the men who built it. In the 1930s, through projects like the caretaker's residence, the WPA gave unemployed workers a second chance, enabling them to earn a paycheck, to learn job skills, and to preserve their self-esteem. They eventually returned to private-sector employment, paid taxes, and contributed productively to their community. Decades later, the caretaker's residence had fallen into disrepair and its future was in doubt. Then, just as the WPA benefited Mishawaka during the Great Depression by building the house, Mishawakans returned the favor: saving the home from demolition, restoring it, and returning it to a useful role in the community.

Today, the Mishawaka Reservoir caretaker's residence stands not only as a monument to the Works Progress Administration and the men who built the house. It speaks, too, of the potential for people and buildings to find new purpose, and thus the redemptive power of a second chance.

CHAPTER 11

NORMAIN HEIGHTS: A LIVING MEMORIAL

The Normain Heights subdivision, located northeast of the intersection of North Main Street and McKinley Avenue in Mishawaka, remains an important link to World War II and the social forces of suburbanization and the Baby Boom that shaped the United States and Mishawaka following the war.

During World War II, housing starts across the country were non-existent, and as soldiers began to return, millions of new housing units were needed. Many families had lived with parents or in-laws while husbands and fathers were away, and many had delayed marriage while the war was on. But as the demands of wartime ended, families reunited and wanted their own home, in keeping with the American Dream soldiers had fought to protect. After the war, the government estimated that a ten-year building program of 1.5 million homes per year would be needed to ease the housing crunch. The move to build new homes was furthered by the G.I. Bill, which offered low-interest mortgage loans to veterans. As a result, home ownership increased from 45% to 65% of the population between 1940-1960.

Housing demand was great, and large numbers of homes were built after the war, many in planned suburban communities, rather than in the inner-cities. Typically, developers would buy a tract of farmland and construct streets, install utilities, and build similar homes. The most prominent example of such a postwar, planned community was Levittown, on New York's Long Island. Beginning in 1946, 17,447 homes were constructed there, and parks, community buildings, and commercial areas were included in the community's design. Each nearly identical home was built on similar streets and sold for the same amount. Levittown became a prototype for suburban housing developments across the country.

Mishawaka also was influenced by these postwar housing trends. When Mishawaka veterans returned from the war, they, too, faced an acute housing shortage. In response to discussions about this need, American Legion Post 161 commander Harry Spaeth appointed Hillis Hans chairman of a committee that would address Mishawaka veterans' housing problems. Veterans of Foreign Wars Post 360 appointed a similar committee. These two groups also approached United Rubber Workers Local 65, many of whose members were vets needing housing.

By August 1946 these groups formed Veterans' Homes of Mishawaka, Inc., a non-profit corporation that would acquire and develop land to provide housing for World War II veterans. While the housing was intended for vets, anyone could purchase a home in the subdivision. Homes were sold at cost, saving perhaps $2000 per home.

The organization purchased 80 acres of farmland on the north side of Mishawaka for their housing project. The parcel of land comprised the old William Schmeltz farm and was purchased from A.A. and Gertrude Felton. A $2,499,000 loan began financing for the development and was repaid through sales of lots and homes. The 80-acre property was annexed into Mishawaka on February 3, 1947.

Surveying and construction of sewers and other outside work began in the spring of 1947, and groundbreaking for the first home occurred on November 13, 1947. Building at Normain Heights reached its maximum pace in the summer of 1948, with 268 construction workers, including 111 carpenters, 47 cement foundation workers, 12 plumbers, 2 roofers, and 68 laborers.

The formal dedication was held in October 1948, and construction was completed by 1949.

The veterans housing site included 315 low-to-medium-cost houses. The project included seven streets, all named for World War II battles: Normandy, Ardennes, Palau, Bastogne, Leyte, Saint Lo, and Guam. North Main Street was extended past US 20 to the northern edge of the subdivision, and a 7-acre park (today Normain Park) along US 20 was also developed. Two acres at the intersection of Main and US 20 were kept for commercial use, and one acre on the west side of Main Street was retained for a church of any denomination interested in buying the site.

In a traffic island at the intersection of Guam and Normandy, a marker honored PFC John F. Nagy, a Marine from South Bend who was killed on Guam on July 6, 1944. Nagy symbolized all who sacrificed for others' freedom. The stone read, "In Memorium, PFC John F. Nagy, U.S. Marine Corps, and all those in the armed services who made the supreme sacrifice."

All of the homes built in this veterans housing project from 1947-49 remain today, with only one being moved to another location in the subdivision. Although most houses have been added on to or remodeled, the neighborhood retains its integrity.

Many of the homes' original features are still visible and reflect housing trends of the time of their construction. To avoid a series of identical Levittown-like houses, Normain Heights buyers had a choice of seven designs. Homes had two or three bedrooms, and were either one or two stories. Large picture windows segmented into smaller square windows were a distinguishing original feature and many remain today. All homes were built with Reynolds aluminum siding, one of the early examples in the country of a large housing development built entirely with aluminum siding. Even though there were several standard floorplans, the houses were not prefabricated, as was sometimes the case with veterans' housing intended as short-term relief for the postwar housing crunch. All major components of the houses were built entirely on-site. Even the wood trusses were assembled inside the old Schmeltz barn, and aluminum siding was cut at the

These homes on Normandy Drive show two types of houses available when Normain Heights was constructed. This photo was taken in 1996.

site. Each home had a choice of coal or oil heating and came with a complete kitchen and bathroom. Lot sizes varied somewhat but were typically 50' wide and 125' deep. As part of the purchase price, all homes were landscaped, including grading, top soil, seeding, and two trees per lot. Advertisements touted these features for potential buyers and thus reflect early efforts at large-scale planned housing developments, the forerunners of the subdivisions that today sprawl across the suburban landscape.

Local newspaper ads from 1947-49 encouraged veterans to buy a home in Normain Heights. A home could be purchased for $680 down, with monthly payments of $57. Down payments later were reduced to $330, with $55-63 monthly installments.

In its design and development, Normain Heights reflects the forces that were creating other planned housing projects, like Levittown, and was a forerunner of housing trends that today we take for granted. The fact that Normain Heights was a project directed by veterans mainly for veterans' needs distinguishes it from other housing constructed by for-profit corporations or the government. Mindful of this, the **Enterprise** wrote this epitaph for the Veterans' Homes of Mishawaka, Inc., in December 1949: "In a few short weeks, its work completed, the corporation will dissolve itself. But it will continue to live as an outstanding example of the fact that given the will to do, men of vision and determination can lick any problem they go after."

The Normain Heights subdivision was listed on the National Register of Historic Places in 2002.

Mishawaka veterans helped win World War II for their country. Normain Heights shows that they then returned home, addressed the housing needs of their community, and won a prosperous peace for their families and themselves.

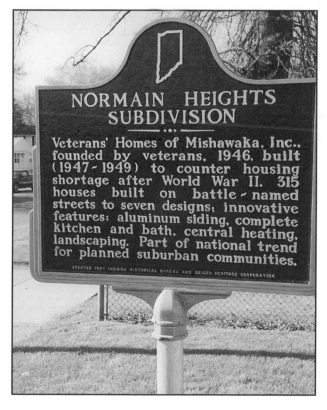

Normain Heights was honored by the Indiana Historical Bureau with an historical marker explaining its significance. It is also listed on the National Register of Historic Places.

CHAPTER 12

LESSONS FROM NORTH SIDE SCHOOL: A PERSONAL ESSAY

Childhood is an amazing time. We spend much of our lives as children trying to leave it behind and much of our adulthood trying to find it again. Our grown-up selves re-experience childhood through our own or others' children, through memories and nostalgia, and, occasionally, by physically returning to the places we knew as children. At some point, each of us has gone back to our earlier selves through one of these means.

The English poet William Wordsworth wrote, "The Child is father of the Man." If we believe that is true, then revisiting our past allows for the opportunity to see both our childhood and adult selves anew. Such vision can be invaluable as we face our adult roles in the present and future. Why do we possess this compelling need to return to our childhood? Maybe we desire the same security, love, freedom, and fun we took for granted in the past. Perhaps we seek a part of our past selves we wish we were more like. It can be healthy to return to part of our past and thus to a part of our present self, a reconciliation of the parts that make us whole.

In May 1992 I had the opportunity to return to North Side School, a building that dominates my memories of childhood. The occasion for

North Side School educated thousands of Mishawaka students until its demolition in 1999.

this return was a tree dedication ceremony in memory of our principal, Mr. Robert Perkins, who died of cancer in 1986. I attended North Side from nursery through sixth grade (1972-1980), but I had not been back inside the building in ten years.

In the parking lot on the rainy Saturday of the dedication, I experienced the first odd clash between my still-strong memories of a child attending school there and the present reality of an adult returning. I had never before driven to the school to go inside. When I was little, I was picked up or dropped off hundreds of times, and I walked to school as I got older. But driving to school always belonged in the unimaginably distant future.

Walking back to the woods behind the school through the soggy, muddy grass, I experienced the start of a curious division in me. While I was certainly standing there in the rain with my family, former teachers, and others participating in the dedication, I also had one foot back in that time long ago when North Side represented a different reality and range of feelings for me as a little boy. I experienced the intensity of the ties that bind us to places in our childhood as I drifted between two times in my life both contained by one place.

The woods carried me back to fall walks in nursery and kinder-garten. We lined up in two rows, one for girls and one for boys. The great honor was to be the "leader" for the day and to thus be at the head of the line. Back in the woods, we all found walking sticks, which we could also use against any of the bears reported to hide in the woods. Identifying any large hole as a definite bear pit, we shuddered to think about being back there at night. I laugh now at the idea of bears living between McKinley Avenue and Day Road-- I never knew where or if the woods had an end in those days-- but those depressions in the ground back in the woods still make me think of what was then so real to us six-year-olds.

Every North Side student remembers the woods behind the school, shown here c. 1994. All of the trees in this photo were destroyed when Liberty School was built on this site in the late 1990s. Other large sections of the woods have since been cleared for new homes and a city well field.

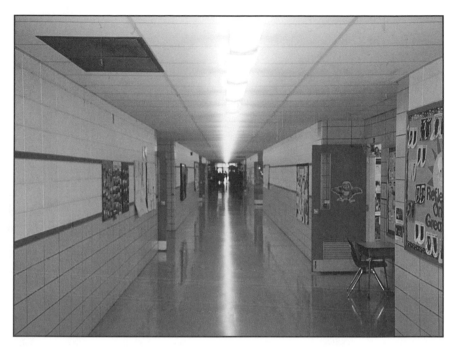

The main hallway of North Side School ran the entire length of the school, from the upper elementary classrooms here to the nursery classroom at the far end.

I am struck now with the question of why I have so few memories of being in the woods as I moved into the older grades. I only remember looking at the woods through the windows of the upper elementary classrooms. Somehow, the turning of the leaves in the fall or feeling the first warm spring day was never the same if we were not outside seeing the collage of color, smelling fallen leaves, or sensing life return as green buds popped out from bare branches.

Memories of the mysteries of the woods behind the school were a prelude to the opportunity to walk through the school, peeking into classrooms and peering back into my past. I felt like I was walking the stage where much of my youth had been played out.

Entering the building near my sixth-grade classrooms, I looked down the long hall that ran the full length of the building, with my nursery classroom at the far end. I had always marveled at the length of that hall, but expected it now to seem shorter because I had grown up. Actually, though, it still seemed a great distance. That, like nearly everything else in the building, had not physically changed at all.

I walked slowly down the hallway through the upper elementary wing. As I peered briefly into darkened classrooms, memories of classes, friends, and teachers surfaced in my thoughts. Outlines of past experiences became colored and vivid in their detail with each step I took.

I was not assailed with quaint thoughts of how simplistic life was then. Instead, I was impressed by the power and lastingness of the memories and experiences. Even though half my life had passed since sixth grade, all that happened during my elementary years was still powerfully present. None of the significance of those events had been diluted by the passage of time or by me growing into adulthood. It was all as meaningful as if it had happened the week before.

My kindergarten room was next as I left the upper elementary behind me. In this class we received paper badges for showing we had mastered basic skills, such as knowing shapes and colors and being able to tie our shoes. I stood before the door, awed that at that spot-- we were tested in the hallway-- 19 years earlier I showed, after much anxiety, that I could tie my shoes. It may seem trivial, but it must be of significance if after all that time my heart still beat faster standing there, fearing the failure of the shoe-tying test.

I soon realized during my walk that most of what called me back to North Side School was in the part of the building where I spent my primary years. This wing, built a decade before the "upper el," contrasted with the wider, shiny light grey floor of the older kids' hall. The primary hall, which was shorter and intersected into the main hall by the principal's office, lacked the false ceiling, fluorescent lights, and bland cinderblocks and thus possessed a warmer, more secure feeling I had not recalled from my time there as a student. Here, the floor was a dark-reddish pattern, students' work lined the ceramic-tiled halls, and real wooden desks and chairs filled the classrooms, unlike the grey metal desks and plastic-backed chairs of the upper el.

Walking past the Quest Center and principal's office, I came finally to the nursery school classroom, which was the first room I entered as a student and the last one on my walk down the long hall. Here, I began my formal schooling twenty years earlier. This was the only room in the school to have really changed. Nursery students no longer attend the Mishawaka schools, so the room had been converted into a computer lab. When I was a student at North Side, not one computer was yet in the building. Instead, we occupied ourselves with such pursuits as building guitars out of shoeboxes and rubber bands, studying Snow White and George Washington, and bringing in our treasures from K-Mart for show-and-tell every week.

My brief return to North Side School gave me renewed access to so much of eight years of my life's experiences and feelings. It allowed my adult perspective to take another look into the childhood that I have come from. As a result of my walk by the woods and from sixth grade back to nursery, I realized that my fondest memories of North Side came in my early years there. I was never aware of that distinction before; I merely saw everything as equal and never sought to look beyond that.

I also can see better now the long-term effect North Side had on the person I am today. In that building I first read and experienced great success and pleasure at learning and came to see my teachers like family members. I speak of them years later with the feeling that I still know them as well as I did when I was their student. They and the atmosphere in the school shaped my desire to be a teacher and to work with students. At North Side, school became a favorite place. Henry Adams said, "A teacher affects eternity," and for those teachers and Mr. Perkins at North Side, that has certainly been true in my experience. This, too, is an understanding I never possessed before that rainy Saturday afternoon, yet it lay there, waiting for North Side to teach me yet another lesson.

French aviator Antoine de Saint-Exupery wrote in **A Sense of Life** about his return as an adult to a park where he used to play games with his friends when he was a child. His adult perspective helps him to realize that he can still reenter the park but not the game he once played. I feel the same way about North Side: I could reenter the school that afternoon, but I can not completely reenter the student, despite the vivid memories I have of that time and place in my life. Nonetheless, I realize that the elementary student who went to school there never really left. He is part of me, continuing to influence me in ways I am still learning to discover.

CHAPTER 13

MISHAWAKA OF THE MOUNTAINS: A PERSONAL ESSAY

After riding about twenty miles from home, I came upon
what I consider the turning point in my life. We came into
a most beautiful spot which seemed to hypnotize me and I
found myself with a longing to stay there...

These words penned by homesteader Walter Thompson describe
how he felt when he first saw his future home, Mishawaka. No,
Thompson was not one of the early settlers of Mishawaka, Indiana, in
the 1830s. Instead, these lines describe his discovery of 160 acres of
mountainous land in northern Colorado in 1916. Thompson had come
west from Mishawaka, Indiana, and was living in Fort Collins-- south-
east of his newly found homestead-- when he made the decision to settle down on the banks of the Cache La Poudre River and create a home
in the wilderness.

On the afternoon of Sunday, July 16, 1995, my father and I, like
Thompson eighty years earlier, found ourselves far from the meander-
ing course of the St. Joseph River and the gentle slopes of the
Mishawaka Hills of our home in Indiana. Instead, as part of our travels in the West, we had already driven nearly 400 miles that day across

the desolation of southern Wyoming's eroded plateaus and valleys, bound for Mishawaka, Colorado.

We had learned of Mishawaka's Western namesake through two articles published in the **South Bend Tribune** in 1992 and 1993 and resolved to include it as a highlight in our quest to see the West. We knew from the articles that Mishawaka, Colorado, was not really a town, not even a small village. Instead, it was described as a bar, restaurant, dance hall, and outdoor amphitheatre, all in one facility along the river, surrounded by mountains, at an elevation of over 5000 feet. A few cabins were near the Mishawaka Inn, but they supported only a seasonal population of inn employees.

Drawing us to Mishawaka, Colorado, was the fascination of seeing the only other place on Earth that shares its name with the city we call home. We wanted to experience the novelty of being in Mishawaka without being in Indiana, of seeing the name in surroundings unlike the flat, open landscape of St. Joseph County.

Leaving Interstate 25 north of Fort Collins, we traveled west through the small town of Wellington and near, ironically, Laporte, along Colorado 1 and 14. Colorado 14 closely paralleled the Cache La Poudre as it came down through the foothills of the Rockies. While the first few miles off the interstate were across flat land, hills loomed ahead and then blended into the mountains that surrounded the river and Mishawaka.

The blue sky with occasional white clouds presented a perfect day for the 14-mile drive through the Poudre Canyon. The two-lane road wove along the river and the base of the mountains towering over the canyon.

The Cache La Poudre was narrower than our Mishawaka's St. Joseph River, perhaps sixty feet wide at most places. However, this river of mountain run-off was far swifter as it descended from its source. In fact, two dozen rafts and kayaks careened their way down the fast-flowing river as we headed up the canyon to Mishawaka.

Steady traffic was coming at us-- jeeps, trucks, and even buses, carrying boats, supplies, and crews of the recreational fleet plying the Poudre. The departure points for such excursions were at various places upriver, but most seemed to end their voyage near the beginning of the foothills, before the Poudre headed east toward Fort Collins and emptied into the South Platte River.

Several roadside boat launches, parking lots, and campsites of the Roosevelt National Forest were filled with rafters, kayaks, and people watching friends go down river. A couple miles from Mishawaka, a dozen homes comprised Poudre Park. With steep mountainsides leaving little flat ground to build on, it was the closest thing to a town that we saw.

Having observed no signs for our destination, we began to wonder if we were following the wrong directions, until we rounded one of many turns on the route, and there it was: Mishawaka, Colorado.

We first saw the east side of the building with the faded words, "Mishawaka Bar-Food," painted on its aluminum roof. Outside of Indiana, there is only one place in the world where we might see a sign like that. We had arrived.

The Mishawaka Inn is surrounded by the mountains of the Cache La Poudre Canyon.

This sign on the side of the Mishawaka Inn is a reminder we aren't in Indiana anymore.

Walking along the road side of the building, we could see that it had been added on to over the years. The exterior walls of the Mishawaka Inn gave the appearance of an enormous log cabin. The east end of the building was the restaurant/bar. The west end of the building, with the dance hall and pool room, was larger and had a roof of regular brown shingles.

Thrilled that we had finally arrived, we took pictures and video outside the building to record the visit. Dozens of cars were parked in the narrow lots to either side of the highway, and a concert by John Hartford, a Tennessee folk singer, was underway. A man stood in the middle of the road directing traffic and allowing people to park or pull onto the busy highway. It was the Poudre Canyon equivalent of Grape Road at rush hour.

Near the entrance to the restaurant/bar, was a large blue Mishawaka Inn sign with the river rapids, an owl, a mountain lion, a big-horned sheep, and an antlered deer: animals definitely not part of the Mishawaka, Indiana, landscape.

To the left of the entrance was a large sign board covered with a dozen colored playbills for future acts coming to the Mishawaka Amphitheatre, including The Radiators, Jerry Jeff Walker and the Gonzo Compadres, 10,000 Maniacs, and Los Lobos. These signs included where to buy tickets for the concerts, mentioning Fort Collins and "at Mishawaka."

We entered the restaurant more thrilled than most of the inn's clientele, for our arrival had followed thousands of miles of driving throughout the West. The novelty of again being in Mishawaka impressed us. Inside, the building had a country/mountain atmosphere, including wood-paneled walls and a carved-wood sign welcoming us to Mishawaka. The bar was to the right, and tables and booths filled the rest of the east wing of the building. The left wall of the room had many pictures of performers and other guests who had come to Mishawaka over the years. A glass case was filled with Mishawaka Inn caps, sweatshirts, and t-shirts. One design featured the Poudre River and rafters going past the inn. Another said, "I've had it with work. I'm heading to Mishawaka for a Bud."

A waitress took us to a table in the rear of the restaurant, by large windows overlooking the river rapids and facing toward the steep mountainsides that form the canyon. As we looked out the window, our view would not have been much different than in the days of the pioneer from the Princess City.

The menu featured typical fare like buffalo wings, nachos, burgers, sandwiches, chicken, and steak. What struck our fancy were the Mishawaka Burger and the Mishawaka Mudslide, the two items on the menu given the name of the Inn, or was it to honor the Indiana city?

When the waitress returned, we enthusiastically ordered the Mishawaka Burger and later the Mishawaka Mudslide, a gooey mix of peanut butter, chocolate, fudge, and whipped cream. If it said "Mishawaka" on it, we were going to have it.

As we ate, occasional yells came from the back of the restaurant or the pool room beyond. We overheard people behind us commenting that the Mishawaka Inn had a reputation for being a wild place. Anyone who could drive from Fort Collins or further, up the winding canyon highway, and then back again at night after a few drinks had to have some daring. The place appealed to that spirit.

When we mentioned to the waitress that we were from the Mishawaka in Indiana-- she then noticed our matching Mishawaka, Indiana, t-shirts-- she seemed interested and said she would tell the manager we were there.

As we finished our Mishawaka Mudslides, the manager, Robin Jones, came by our table. Pleased to learn that we had made the trek from Indiana to visit his Mishawaka, he said that in the years since the **Tribune** articles, many people from Indiana had stopped by, which led us to later wonder if the Mishawaka Inn merchandise was intended for Coloradans or for pilgrims from the Princess City. Jones told us he had been to Mishawaka and mentioned a visit to the Mishawaka Brewing Company on North Main Street. He then invited us onto the patio, where John Hartford was finishing his concert in the outdoor amphitheatre.

After our dessert, we headed out back, where Hartford was singing

The Poudre River is a favorite of rafters, offering a scenic view for customers of the Mishawaka Inn, at right.

to a crowd of three hundred, seated around small white tables. The area had wooden fencing along the sides of the amphitheatre facing the road and a wooded area west of the property. To the east was the back of the inn, where a few people sat at tables with drinks or food.

What made the whole scene so spectacular was that along the north side of the amphitheatre the river rushed and swirled through the mountainous scene. The manager informed us he was trying to get one of the mountains overlooking the inn, named Mishawaka Mountain. This beautiful setting was bathed in the late afternoon sunlight, which glistened off the water and intensified the blue sky, as well as deepening the green of the mountains' pine trees.

As proud supporters of Mishawaka-- regardless of the state-- we were pleased to hear Hartford refer to Mishawaka in his performance. Also, a large banner at the rear of the amphitheatre welcomed Hartford and his audience to Mishawaka.

Hartford finished his performance by encouraging audience members to come forward for some fiddle-playing and square dancing. Walter Thompson would have been pleased to see people enjoying music and dancing in the Poudre Canyon. He, his wife, and their children were all musicians and operated a dance hall at Mishawaka in the summers, the origins of the Mishawaka Amphitheatre.

We paused to enjoy the moment of being in a Mishawaka surrounded by incredible mountain scenery. For a while, we experienced what had attracted Thompson decades before: a paradise of mountains, forests, rushing river currents, and soothing sunlight-- all well removed from the nearest city. Such a place could only have one name: Mishawaka.

Throughout the three hours that we spent in Mishawaka, we felt we belonged, as if we had a claim to this Mishawaka of the mountains by right of our ties to the "mother city" back in Indiana.

As we wound our way back down the Poudre Canyon and east toward the Mishawaka of our home, we left a Mishawaka that is a worthy bearer of its name. It was satisfying to know that the name "Mishawaka" had been spread to such a beautiful place, that it was spoken by thousands of people each year, and that this colony of the Princess City prospered, fulfilling the vision of its founder.

Part III

EVENTS

CHAPTER 14

⚜

REVEREND BILLY SUNDAY'S
LAST ALTAR CALL

The foremost evangelist of the first half of the twentieth century, the Reverend Billy Sunday, of Winona Lake, Indiana, spoke to approximately one hundred million people during his forty-year religious career. The Iowa-born, former Chicago White Stockings base stealer warned that urbanism, immigration, and liberalism threatened America's moral character. Sunday preached that the cure to these ills could be found in repentance, salvation, Bible study, prayer, church attendance, sexual purity, and abstinence from alcohol and drugs.

Two books offer insight into Billy Sunday's life and ministry: **Ma Sunday Still Speaks** and Lyle W. Dorsett's **Billy Sunday and the Redemption of Urban America**.

Sunday was one of the best known men in America at the height of his career, between 1908-1920, when he led enormous revivals in major cities throughout the country. In 1913 his seven-week crusade in South Bend and Mishawaka drew tens of thousands of both faithful and curious.

In the 1920s and 1930s, though, Sunday's ministry was challenged by his health problems, family tragedies, and financial concerns. Also, the cultural climate of the Roaring Twenties made the country less

*The First United Methodist Church, shown here c. 1930, was the site of
Reverend Billy Sunday's final sermon.*

receptive to his message, and he conducted no more extended revivals
in large cities. Billy Sunday continued to preach, but more often in
smaller cities and towns. Rather than using his specially built wooden
tabernacles that could seat thousands, Sunday spoke in churches, with
crowds of 500-1000 people.

With his ministry reduced in scope, Sunday preached until ten days
before his death in November 1935 at age 72. The final chapter of
Sunday's ministry was written at Mishawaka's First United Methodist
Church, where the evangelist gave his last sermon on October 27,
1935.

Homer Rodeheaver, Sunday's music director during the great urban
revivals, had been assisting Rev. Samuel H. Turbeville of the First
United Methodist Church during a two-week "religious crusade" in the
latter part of October. As the Sundays were preparing to leave their
Winona Lake cottage for a visit to Nell "Ma" Sunday's brother in
Chicago, their friend Rodeheaver drove up and asked if Rev. Sunday

could preach the next night in Mishawaka, because Rodeheaver had to leave suddenly to attend to business in Washington, DC.

Mindful that Sunday had been recovering from a heart attack since May, Rodeheaver said, "I thought maybe, if you were feeling better, you would like to go and try yourself out in the service."

Sunday answered, "Oh, yes, I would like to. I am feeling better!"

His wife was critical of the idea, knowing Sunday had not preached since May and had not been feeling well: "Now, dad, don't say you'll go. You know the doctor told you you shouldn't, and you weren't able to."

Rev. Sunday would not hear of this, and angrily pounded the table, "I guess I know how I feel!"

Ma Sunday could only reply, "All right, if that's the way you want it, we'll go."

By Thursday evening, October 24, word had reached Mishawaka that Sunday would be appearing at the First United Methodist Church on Friday. Because of the huge crowds Sunday was expected to draw, loudspeakers were placed in the Sunday school room and social rooms in the church basement, to bring Sunday's preaching to a crowd of more than 2000 people.

At 6 PM already there was not a seat to be had in the sanctuary for the 7:30 PM service. Ma Sunday later remembered, "The church was literally packed with people-- chairs in every aisle, on the platform, on the steps, and every place. People sat even under the pianos and all over the platform. There wasn't room to step beside the pulpit where Billy stood."

Ma Sunday spoke introductory remarks to the 2000 people who filled the church to hear Billy Sunday. The **South Bend Tribune** reported that Rev. Sunday's theme was from II Kings 4:26: "'Run now I pray thee, to meet her and say unto her, Is it well with thee? Is it well with thy husband? Is it well with thy child? And she answered, It is well.'" He also warned "people to flee from the wrath to come."

Throughout Sunday's career, a popular feature of his evangelism was the "altar call." After the sermon or program was concluded, Sunday would ask people to come forward, to take his hand, and to express or renew their commitment to follow Christ. This was always a highlight of the service for Sunday.

Ma Sunday recalled that at the Friday service, "it was so crowded that when Billy gave the invitation only one person got through to shake his hand. So, the meeting had to be dismissed."

Before the service was concluded, according to Ma Sunday, her husband "whispered to the preacher, 'I'll come back Sunday night and preach for you again,'" to conclude the religious revival.

After the Friday service, the **Tribune** noted that despite Sunday's age and recent ill health, he "retains much of his vigor and pep" shown in South Bend in 1913. When speaking in Mishawaka, Rev. Sunday also used his characteristic "old baseball gestures" and humor, keeping "his audience in laughter much of the time."

Interestingly, though, ten days later, the Associated Press gave a contradictory impression of Sunday's performance in Mishawaka: "His

Billy Sunday spoke from this altar to conclude the First United Methodist Church's religious crusade.

The congregation of the First United Methodist Church erected this plaque to honor the historic event that occurred there in 1935.

preaching there had lost some of its fire. He didn't take off his coat and vest nor start the famous pitching 'windup' he had used on revival rostrums for 39 years."

Perhaps because of a rainy evening, the crowd two days later was smaller, but still an enormous 1500. Sunday's theme came from Acts 16:30: "' Sirs, what must I do to be saved?'" This question was asked by the Philippian jailer following Paul and Silas' escape. Paul's response to the question was, "'Believe in the Lord Jesus Christ and thou shalt be saved.'"

The **Tribune** account of the sermon said Sunday also explained how both Biblical prophets and modern ministers face temptation. Sunday said, "One time I was grievously tempted. Millionaires from New York laid down a check for $50,000 if I would consent to appear as an evangelist in a motion picture, promising $1,000,000. I said 'God saved me from sin. He has given me what reputation I have and my life is dedicated to His work. But I thank you for the offer.' It was a great temptation but I was no Harold Lloyd, Mae West, or a Marlene Dietrich."

As part of the evening's activities, the congregation presented Rev. Sunday with the yellow chair he used during his evangelical crusade in South Bend in 1913. The **Tribune** noted that Sunday both sat and stood on the chair, enjoying his recollections of the revival in South Bend and Mishawaka. This chair is today on display in the Northern Indiana Center for History.

Over 1000 of the audience stood with Sunday to profess they were Christians. According to Ma Sunday, more than 40 people then came forward to the altar when Sunday invited them to express their desire to be converted to Christ. She remembered, "It thrilled his heart." During forty years of preaching, approximately a million faithful came forward in Sunday's altar calls. The last of those were in Mishawaka.

The **Tribune** article concluded, "The services Sunday evening will linger long in the memory of Mishawaka from every religious denomination."

The following week, the Sundays went to Chicago, as originally planned. There, on November 6, 1935, Billy Sunday suffered another heart attack, and died shortly after.

Almost 70 years after his death, Rev. Billy Sunday is still seen as one of the most influential Americans of his time and an important figure in the history of religion in America. A tangible part of his legacy can be found today in Winona Lake at the Billy Sunday Home and Visitor Center.

CHAPTER 15

ON THE BRINK: SHELBY SHAKE AND JOHNNY WOODEN

The 1936-37 Mishawaka High School basketball season was unlike any in Mishawaka's long and rich sports tradition. The season saw the Cavemen go from rags to riches on the hardwood and Coach Shelby S. Shake make a mistake he would pay for the rest of his life.

Coach Shake

Shake was born and raised near Eminence, in Morgan County, southwest of Indianapolis. He graduated from Eminence High School and Indiana State University and was a World War I infantry veteran. Shake was a teacher and head basketball coach at Cloverdale High School for two years. In 1923, at age 27, he came to Mishawaka as a woodshop and commercial math teacher, becoming head basketball coach in 1924.

Shelby Shake was coaching his eleventh season at Mishawaka, where his teams had won four sectional championships-- the most recent in 1935-- and a regional in 1927. The first coach to use Mishawaka's new gymnasium, Shake had developed Mishawaka into a perennial power, especially at tourney time. Arthur Vallicelli, a senior co-captain on the '37 team, remembered, "Shake was a good guy, very dedicated. I liked him very much. He was a good coach. There was no question about it. He was a student of the game." Robert Schweisberger, a sophomore on the team, described Shake as "pretty strict," but "he stuck up for the boys real good."

Vallicelli also recalled Shake's rigorous practices and firm discipline, keys to the program's success: "He was very demanding. When you practiced, you practiced. There was never any monkeying around." The Cavemen practiced in-bounds and shooting plays for hours, until "you could do it in your sleep," Vallicelli noted. "The team was trained to obey orders. Everyone knew what the others were doing. Shake was a stubborn guy. You did it his way."

Van Norris, a sophomore reserve, remembered practicing Shake's complex offense: "Shake insisted on us learning how to do a figure eight...One of the most difficult things you can do in basketball." The figure eight movement put all the offensive players in motion, passing

Shelby Shake, shown here in the 1926 Mishawaka High School Miskodeed, coached the Cavemen into the Sweet Sixteen state finals the next year.

The 1937 Miskodeed included this photo of Coach Shake preparing the team for one of their opponents.

the ball and looking for an open shot.

In his years at the Mishawaka helm, Shake also enjoyed a reputation as a showman, employing tactics that inspired his team and intimidated opponents. His 1927 team went to the Sweet Sixteen state finals wearing unique vertical-striped uniforms, and the '37 team debuted the school's first black silk uniforms. At the first Mishawaka home game in November 1936, another one of Shake's gimmicks was introduced to northern Indiana basketball fans: the Bask-O-Lite. After each basket, a red light mounted behind the rim would flash and lights above the backboard would display the word **GOAL**. Shake's players remember the intimidating effect the device had on opponents who were not used to it.

The Incident

The 1936-37 Maroons returned several players off a team that went 16-8 and lost by one point to Riley in the championship game of the

1936 Mishawaka sectional. Instead of returning to the successful form of the previous season, the Cavemen soon dropped to 5-11 and rode a four-game losing streak into their January 29 rematch with Northern Indiana High School Conference foe South Bend Central. Central had bested Shake's team in their first meeting, 35-34, in South Bend. The Bears' first-year coach was former Purdue All-American Johnny Wooden.

This contest, fought before a capacity crowd of over 2000 fans at Mishawaka High School, would eventually be known across the state and would have profound repercussions for the Mishawaka basketball program and perhaps even the sport of basketball.

After a close first half, the Cavemen took a six-point lead into half-time, but saw it slip away in the final minutes of the game, as Central again defeated Mishawaka, 36-32. The **South Bend Tribune** described the intense contest with warfare imagery: "a heated hardwood battle...as fiery a skirmish as the teams have ever unfolded in their bitter, ancient rivalry."

This loss eliminated Mishawaka as a contender for the conference championship. Also, for the first time in 13 years, Mishawaka had lost to Central twice in the same season, a fact that would have been difficult for Coach Shake to accept. Vallicelli recalled, "He was prone to want to win at any cost. That was his problem."

Shake, known for his fiery temper, occasional profane language, and colorful courtside antics, succumbed to his emotions and frustration after the game was over. As he met Wooden at mid-floor, the Mishawaka coach accused, "How much did you pay those officials?"

Wooden later alleged that Shake used profanity and called Wooden a name which sent the Central coach rushing at Shake, trying to land a punch. The crowd standing nearby interceded before the two could actually come to blows.

Cavemen senior co-captain Art Van Tone observed the scuffle from the door of the Mishawaka locker room. In the crowd standing around and between Shake and Wooden, Van Tone saw what he thought was a boy wearing a Central letter sweater holding on to Shake. According to the **Tribune** account, Van Tone, trying to defend his coach from

The Mishawaka High School gymnasium is pictured here at the time of the new building's completion in 1924. Shelby Shake and John Wooden had their infamous altercation here on January 29, 1937.

what he thought was a mob, "dove into the pile and put on a flying block that knocked down more persons than any punches swung before or since the dispute had opened."

Van Norris recalled, "It was a surprise that it ever happened. We couldn't believe it."

Cooler heads soon prevailed, and later Shake and Wooden shook hands. The Mishawaka coach blamed his outburst on the emotions of the contest. He told a **Tribune** reporter that night that he was sorry about the incident and preferred just to forget about it.

In 2000 John Wooden shared his perspective on the confrontation with Shake: "He lost his head over losing a close game at home and made remarks for which he was sorry. He apologized to me the next day and I thought that was the end of it."

The schools' principals had more to say publicly about the fracas, none of it positive about Shelby Shake. Central principal P.D. Pointer said, "I think it was a disgraceful exhibition on the part of Shake. His language was terrible and he proved definitely that he's a hard loser. I'm proud of the way Johnny Wooden acted. He was a gentleman at all times." He added, "I will accept Mr. Shake's apology for his conduct and consider the affair a closed incident."

Mishawaka principal Charles Kern said, "I never was so embarrassed in my life." He added his appreciation for Pointer's understanding and expressed his desire that the schools continue their athletic relations without further problems. South Bend Central and Mishawaka had a history of trouble in their rivalry, most notably a 1920 fight at a football game that resulted in the schools not playing each other for two years.

Modern-day high school basketball fans may be surprised at Shake's comment about Wooden, the visiting coach, paying officials. Today, officials for regular season games are hired by the home team, and it is visiting fans who often talk about officials being paid by the home school as part of the home-court advantage.

The origins of the incident go back to the previous year when officials' contracts for 1936-37 games were being signed. Then Central coach Ralph Parmenter agreed to use the Riley athletic director as an official for the Mishawaka--Central game. When Wooden took over the Central program in the fall of 1936, he objected to a South Bend administrator officiating a game between Mishawaka and any South Bend school. Both Shake and Wooden agreed to substitute Al Berkey, an Elkhart assistant coach, along with Charles Bennett, a referee from LaPorte.

Ironically, the near-fight between Shake and Wooden was a family feud, of sorts. Howard Shake, Coach Shake's cousin, says Johnny Wooden's and Shelby Shake's grandmothers were Yager sisters, making the coaches second cousins. Howard Shake remembered Shelby's mother giving her perspective on the incident: "'Things like this happen when two hot-headed Yagers get together.'" Shelby Shake was also a cousin of Glenn Curtiss, Wooden's former high school basketball coach at Martinsville. Much of Shake's basketball strategy had come from Curtiss' state champion Artesian program.

Shake did not speak with his players about his actions on January 29, according to Vallicelli: "Shake was very close. He would not talk about that."

The next week Indiana High School Athletic Association executive secretary Arthur L. Trester began a probe of the incident. He ordered written statements from both schools' coaches and principals. By Friday, February 6, it seemed the matter would be resolved without further action by the IHSAA. Kern received a letter from Trester that stated, "If the matter can be settled at your end of the line it will be appreciated by the I.H.S.A.A."

Shake was called before the Mishawaka school board, to whom he expressed regret and promised to control his actions in the future. The school board reprimanded him, and the matter was considered closed.

Tourney Time

In February local basketball teams and fans focused more on the games at hand and the impending sectional tourney, rather than on the actions of Coach Shelby Shake.

Schweisberger observed that Shake "stressed pretty good defense...In those days it was more or less a controlled game. Not many shots were taken." Part of the slow pace of the game in that era came from having a jump ball after each field goal, a rule Indiana discontinued after the 1936-37 season. While Shake was normally a believer in screens, blocks, and set plays, that season Mishawaka struggled to find a good guard combination and had nobody taller than six feet, Vallicelli explained. As the season wore on, though, Shake solved his guard problem and switched to a fast-break offense, telling his team, "We don't have the height, but we have the speed and ball-handling.'" Shake followed the lead of many college coaches who were experimenting with the fast break that season. With what the **Tribune** dubbed the new "firewagon style" offensive scheme, the hot Maroons destroyed their last two regular season opponents.

Despite an 8-14 record, Mishawaka entered the twelve-team Mishawaka sectional as one of the favorites, along with Central and Lakeville.

The 1936–37 Mishawaka Cavemen basketball team
top: Carl Norris, Charles Robison, Richard Good, Olen Parks, Jack Ulery
middle: Paul Vander Heyden, Charles Van Paris, Arthur Van Tone, George
Miukluk, Rudolph Meuninck, Donald Moore, Arthur Vallicelli, Robert
Dentino
front: Van Norris, Robert Schweisberger, Stanley Ciszczon, Roy Bolen,
George Marzotto, Edward Grant, Joe Gall, Lee Savage, Joseph Gerard

Local basketball fans-- especially Cavemen-- longed to see a rematch between Central and Mishawaka. The **Tribune** observed, "If Central and the Maroons are paired...tickets will be sought at premium prices for much ill-will exists between the rival squads... Mishawaka would not be at all adverse to an opportunity to avenge two close losses to the Orange and Blue."

In another preview article during sectional week, the **Tribune** commented on the implications of Mishawaka's new offensive scheme: "Shelby Shake has switched to the fast break in the past two weeks which means that Central and Mishawaka will present the same style of offensive play. With Shake and Johnny Wooden fast-breaking up and down the sidelines the contest would be even more enjoyable."

As Shake prepared his team for their first sectional opponent, Riley, a possible showdown with Central must have been on his mind as well.

Mishawaka defeated Riley 41-35, setting up the semi-final with Central. Before the game, Shake did not talk to his team about revenge. Instead, Vallicelli remembered Shake told them, "This was your last game if you don't win.'" Each player knew the path to the sectional title lay through Central. South Bend led into the third quarter, but the Cavemen pulled out the dramatic 41-39 victory. The **Tribune** saw Mishawaka's win after two earlier defeats by the Bears as proof of the "Hoosier hoodoo": "you can't beat a major opponent three times in the same season."

While he may not have expressed it to his team, how sweet must have been the feeling for Shelby Shake to defeat Wooden and the Bears, ending their season on the same court where the disappointing January 29 loss and its embarrassing aftermath had occurred. It was one of the most satisfying Mishawaka wins of the Shake era.

One final obstacle to a sectional championship for Mishawaka was the 26-0 Lakeville Trojans, who had beaten the Cavemen early in the season, at Mishawaka. This time, the tired Mishawakans overcame an early deficit to defeat Lakeville, 44-38. Shake again used his fast-break offense with great success. The **Tribune** noted with amazement the high point totals Mishawaka amassed in the sectional: 126 points in three games, a 42-point average.

It was a sectional tourney to remember. The **Tribune's** Arthur Johnson described it as "the most heated sectional basketball tournament ever unfolded in St. Joseph county." The **South Bend News-Times** reported that all records for attendance at the Mishawaka sectional were broken in 1937.

The **News-Times** noted the often-volatile Shake's behavior during the pressure-packed championship game: "Shelby S. Shake, Mishawaka cage mentor, was cool as a cucumber during the entire proceedings. He sat in the same seat throughout the entire game. Coming back for the second half he made a lad move over so he could keep the same seat. Superstitious?"

In the first game of the Rochester regional the next week, Mishawaka faced NIHSC-champion Elkhart. At 22-3, the Blazers were heavily favored to win the regional, and a contender for the state championship. Mishawaka placed its hopes on Shake's offense and the "Hoosier hoodoo," having lost twice already to the Blue Blazers.

In one of the biggest upsets in local basketball history, the Cavemen sent Elkhart home early, 28-23. The Blazers made the first basket of the game, but never led Mishawaka again. Shake's fast-break offense, screen plays, and the tight Maroon defense frustrated Elkhart's hopes.

In the championship game against Rochester, Mishawaka picked up where it left off against Elkhart and sprinted to a 10-2 lead. The Zebras gradually wore Mishawaka down, though, and then outplayed the tired Cavemen to come out on top, 29-26. Rochester later advanced to the state finals before losing to eventual state champion Anderson.

Despite the disappointing loss, Mishawaka's season had been amazing. As the Maroons left the court, their faithful cheered a team that had battled from mediocrity to greatness, repeatedly playing the role of victorious underdog in the state tourney.

What nobody knew that night in Rochester was that it would be the last basketball game Shelby Shake would ever coach.

The "Recommendation"

After the loss to Rochester in the regional championship game, the community had little reason to think about the January 29 altercation between Shake and Wooden. This would have been to Shake's liking, as he wanted to forget his moment of indiscretion that almost led to a fistfight with the Central mentor.

The matter of Shake's actions after the loss to Central would not be closed, though.

Officials from both schools were told to attend an April 10 hearing in Indianapolis before Arthur Trester, secretary of the Indiana High School Athletic Association, and its Board of Control.

On April 13 letters from the IHSAA were received by the principals of both Mishawaka and Central. The letters read:

Recognition is given to the attempt made by Principals Kern and Pointer to secure wholesome athletic conditions in their schools in the past and they are requested to continue past efforts to the end that high standards in athletics may be maintained.

The board of control unanimously recommends that Coach Shelby Shake of Mishawaka be relieved of all duties and responsibilities connected with athletic activities and that a letter to this effect be signed by members of the school board, superintendent and high school principal of Mishawaka and sent to the I.H.S.A.A. at an early date.

A.L. Trester
Commissioner

Shelby Shake read Trester's letter in Principal Kern's office and went home, knowing that the "recommendation" was in fact an order that his coaching at Mishawaka was over.

Mishawaka was given little leeway in response to the IHSAA's letter. It could either fire Shake or essentially cease interscholastic competition. If Mishawaka would have resisted the "recommendation," it would have been suspended from the IHSAA, which meant other IHSAA member schools would have been unable to schedule Mishawaka in any sport.

The IHSAA decision not only meant that Shake would lose his basketball job at Mishawaka, but it also was essentially a lifetime ban on Shake ever coaching at any Indiana high school. The **South Bend Tribune** reported the reality of the situation succinctly when it broke the news: "Arthur Trester's ax fell on Shelby Shake's neck today."

Vallicelli described his thoughts on the IHSAA order: "It was unfortunate." Believing that Shake had been treated unfairly, the team offered to protest: "We did talk about it. We were willing to go to bat for him."

Shake, though, told them, "'Absolutely not. I'll be leaving in a quiet way.'"

Vallicelli added, "It just died right there."

The next day, Shelby Shake turned in his teaching and coaching resignation to the Mishawaka school board, effective at the end of the school year. Recognizing the inevitable, Shake thus avoided making Mishawaka High School choose between defending him or keeping its sports program intact.

"He was a real good basketball coach...I was sorry to see him leave," recollected Schweisberger.

John Wooden remembered, "I was very sorry for Mr. Shake and did not know that he had previously had some problems with his temper."

Shake's resignation did not end the controversy. Newspapers from Mishawaka and South Bend all the way to Evansville expressed their opinions on the IHSAA's "recommendation."

James Costin, sports editor of the **South Bend News-Times**, wrote, "Arthur Trester...has wandered far afield in ordering Shake to give up coaching...We fail to see why Trester should be offended to such an extent that he found it necessary to bar Shake as a coach in this state for the rest of his life. If Shake were such a disreputable character, it seems strange that Shake's superiors in the Mishawaka school system...didn't find it out for 14 years-- and then from a man who hadn't even seen Shake in a year's time."

Mishawaka's **Fair Dealer** was far more pointed in its sentiments. Beginning with reference to the "dictatorial power of the Mussolini of Indiana high school athletics, Arthur L. Trester," the paper also noted Shake's "sportsmanship" for saving the school board the difficult decision of whether to fire him and "the raw deal he had received."

Keeping in mind Mishawaka's victories over both Riley and Central en route to the sectional title, the **Fair Dealer** blamed "somebody from South Bend" for resurrecting the January 29 incident and bringing it again to Trester's attention. Bitterly, the paper said, "Perhaps if Coach Shake had arranged to lose the sectional tourney instead of making such a fine showing, all would have been forgiven as well as forgotten."

What about Coach Wooden? Should he have been punished for his involvement in the argument with Shake? The **Fair Dealer** referred to Wooden going unreprimanded as "cock-eyed justice." Its front-page editorial hinted that Shake was not the only one to blame: "It takes two to make a bargain, whether it be a good bargain or a bad one, or whether it be for good or evil...Both coaches had felt the tenseness of straining nerves."

Shelby Shake's fate exposed an issue that affected every high school in Indiana: the power of Arthur Trester and the IHSAA.

Jack Ledden, sports editor of the **Tribune**, described the "powerful club" of "Czar Trester" and how firmly entrenched in power he was, thanks to the many small schools whose voting power dominated the IHSAA.

In words reminiscent of the class sports debate in the 1990s, Ledden suggested that the large schools north of Lafayette and Fort Wayne could withdraw from the IHSAA and form their own tournaments. He said, "About 130 good high schools banding together would crush the backbone of Trester's organization and keep athletics on even keel. It's worth trying."

The **Evansville Press** did not excuse Shake's actions, but was more concerned about the power exercised by the IHSAA in disciplining the Mishawaka coach. It advocated local control over hiring and firing coaches, rather than the "dictatorial power" of "Boss" Trester and the IHSAA board of control: "When an outside organization...a group of men from here, there, and over there in Indiana can step into any one community and say this or that man cannot be retained as basketball coach then the IHSAA is overstepping itself. It's getting too far out on the limb and covering far too much territory."

No change resulted from Shelby Shake's case and all of the hand-wringing about the power of Trester and the IHSAA. No secession of northern schools from the association occurred.

Perhaps the final written statement about the Shake controversy came from the 1937 **Miskodeed**, Mishawaka High School's yearbook. While not referring to the post-game events of January 29, Trester, or Shake's removal, the Mishawaka students made their defiant statement about Shake at the start of the article about the basketball season: "Coach Shelby S. Shake drilled his boys thoroughly in the fundamentals of the game, but he also stressed fine sportsmanship. Clean and fair playing was conspicuously evident in all games, regardless of score."

The three main participants in the Shake--Wooden--Trester controversy went on to varied fates.

Arthur L. Trester died in 1944, and since 1945 the IHSAA has given the Trester Mental Attitude Award to a senior in the boys basketball state finals.

Johnny Wooden stayed at South Bend Central for nine seasons, compiling a 218-42 record. He coached two seasons at Indiana State and 27 years at UCLA. At UCLA Wooden amassed a 620-147 record, winning 10 NCAA championships before his retirement in 1975. He was inducted into the Indiana Basketball Hall of Fame and the Naismith Basketball Hall of Fame. Wooden is widely regarded as the greatest basketball coach of all time.

The Shake incident presents one of the great what-ifs of sports history. If the IHSAA had reprimanded or even fired Wooden for trying to punch Shake, how might Wooden's career have been affected? Would colleges have been reluctant to hire him with such a black mark on his record? Would UCLA have won its championships without Wooden as coach? How would the fates of dozens of UCLA players have been affected if the Wooden dynasty had never been?

Shelby Shake left Mishawaka holding several school records, including most wins (141-114) and most winning seasons (8). In just eleven years, Shake's teams won one regional and five sectional championships. It took 49 more seasons for Shake's Cavemen successors, combined, to equal his total of sectional and regional titles.

Shake taught briefly in Indianapolis and at Eastern Illinois University. He then moved to Carbondale, Illinois, where he was an assistant professor of industrial education at Southern Illinois University. He never again coached high school basketball. Shake died in 1962 and is buried in Paris, Illinois.

In 1999 Shelby Shake was inducted into the Mishawaka High School Athletic Hall of Fame.

Mishawaka High School Basketball

Season Record (12-15)
1936-37

Mishawaka	20	Bourbon	23
Mishawaka	28	Lakeville	33
Mishawaka	30	Nappanee	24
Mishawaka	33	Goshen	28
Mishawaka	34	S.B. Central	35
Mishawaka	33	S.B. Riley	26
Mishawaka	20	Muncie	26
Mishawaka	31	Hammond	44
Mishawaka	30	S.B. Riley	40
Mishawaka	31	Brazil	26
Mishawaka	32	T.H. Garfield	33
Mishawaka	23	Nappanee	22
Mishawaka	25	Rochester	36
Mishawaka	22	S.B. Riley	28 (OT)
Mishawaka	20	Elkhart	28
Mishawaka	20	LaPorte	42
Mishawaka	32	S.B. Central	36
Mishawaka	43	Michigan City	21
Mishawaka	14	Elkhart	26
Mishawaka	22	Winamac	23
Mishawaka	44	Culver	24
Mishawaka	35	S.B. Washington	24

Sectional (Mishawaka)

Mishawaka	41	S.B. Riley	35
Mishawaka	41	S.B. Central	39
Mishawaka	44	Lakeville	38

Regional (Rochester)

Mishawaka	28	Elkhart	23
Mishawaka	26	Rochester	29

CHAPTER 16

SLAPPED BY PATTON

More than 4000 people from Mishawaka served in the armed forces during World War II. Among them was Private Charles H. Kuhl, who unwillingly became a participant in an incident that affected the career of one of America's most important generals and perhaps altered the outcome of the war in Europe.

Carlo D'Este's biography **Patton: A Genius for War** and Stephen Ambrose's **Americans at War** provide much insight on this topic.

In the summer of 1943, the 27-year-old Kuhl was in General George S. Patton's Seventh Army, which was engaged in an arduous, month-long campaign to wrest control of Sicily from the Germans and Italians, in preparation for the invasion of the Italian peninsula. Narrow mountain roads, strong German defenses, and the dust and heat of summer added to the difficulty Patton faced in his drive to be the first to take Messina, the prize sought by both Patton and the British Eighth Army. The Allies took Sicily, but only after the Axis forces successfully withdrew to the Italian mainland. The campaign frustrated General Patton, and he wrote that he was eager "to get out of this infernal Island."

On the afternoon of August 3, Patton made one of his frequent hospital visitations, this time to the 15th Evacuation Hospital near Nicosia. As Patton made his rounds among the wounded soldiers, he came across Private Kuhl, a 1st Division infantryman who showed no apparent wound or injury.

In a 1970 interview with the **South Bend Tribune**, Kuhl remembered that when Patton entered the hospital tent "all the soldiers jumped to attention except me. I was suffering from battle fatigue and just didn't know what to do."

After asking each soldier what his injury was, Patton questioned Kuhl why he had not stood and saluted. Kuhl explained to the **Tribune**, "I told him my nerves were shot and of course I didn't feel like getting up to salute him." D'Este and Ambrose report Kuhl's words differently, a simple "I guess I can't take it."

The furious general began swearing at Kuhl, referring to him as a coward, and ordered that he leave the hospital tent. The frightened Kuhl did not move, which only enraged Patton more. According to an eyewitness, the general then "slapped [Kuhl's] face with a glove, raised him to his feet by the collar of his shirt and pushed him out of the tent with a final 'kick in the rear.'"

Patton ordered the private to return to his unit and told the doctors, "Don't admit this son of a bitch. I don't want yellow-bellied bastards like him hiding their lousy cowardice around here, stinking up this place of honor!"

Kuhl fled the tent and hid until Patton left the hospital. Kuhl then returned and was admitted for acute anxiety, chronic diarrhea, malaria, and a high fever.

That night Patton wrote in his diary about the slapping incident, referring to Kuhl as "the only arrant coward I have ever seen in this army." He expressed that soldiers claiming battle fatigue-- a condition Patton did not consider legitimate-- who "shirk their duty...should be tried for cowardice and shot." He added, "One sometimes slaps a baby to bring it to."

Two days later, Patton ordered that Seventh Army soldiers alleging shell-shock would not be admitted to hospitals and that those who refused to fight would be court-martialed "for cowardice in the face of the enemy."

On August 10 Patton visited the 93rd Evacuation Hospital and again came across an unwounded soldier, Private Paul Bennett, who claimed his nerves made him unable to fight. Patton swore at Bennett, called him a coward, and waved a pistol in front of the soldier, threatening to shoot him. Patton then twice struck Private Bennett.

While the slapping incidents soon became widely known in Sicily, it was not until later in the year that the media back in the United States began to report what had occurred.

Realizing that striking an enlisted man was a court-martial offense, General Eisenhower, Patton's commander, needed to both punish Patton and prevent the incidents from causing a stir back home. He feared that such a backlash would result in Patton being relieved of command. Eisenhower would thus lose a general whom he felt was "indispensable to the war effort-- one of the guarantors of our victory."

Part of Patton's punishment for the slappings was a strong censure in which Eisenhower said he could not "excuse brutality, abuse of the sick, nor exhibition of uncontrollable temper in front of subordinates." Eisenhower also said he now questioned Patton's "good judgment and self-discipline," and ordered Patton to publicly apologize for his actions.

On August 22 Patton summoned to Palermo all the witnesses of the slappings. In his attempt to apologize, Patton explained to the soldiers that he had acted out of a desire to help the shell-shocked soldiers recover more quickly by having them be motivated by anger toward Patton. He noted a World War I comrade who had suffered from mental problems during the war and committed suicide. Patton believed that a strong response from a commander could have prevented the soldier's death. Many witnesses of the apology saw it more as a justification for the actions than as an expression of contrition.

Patton also personally apologized to Kuhl. He told the private that his slapping and verbal abuse were intended to motivate Kuhl to think, "I'll show that SOB Patton that I am not a yellow coward, become brave and redeem myself." Patton then admitted, "But I see now that I used the wrong psychology," and added, "If you will shake my hand in forgiveness, I'll be much obliged to you." An observer noted that Kuhl grinned enthusiastically and shook Patton's hand.

Kuhl felt that Patton "was suffering a little battle fatigue himself" when the slapping occurred, a view that Patton biographer D'Este agrees with. While Patton rejected the idea of battle fatigue in his men, today psychologists and the military know much more about this mental condition. As a result of the enormous stresses of the drive to Messina, two years of intense planning and training, and the fighting in North Africa, Patton was not in the best mental condition on August 3, 1943. Also, the day before Kuhl was slapped, Patton had visited a field hospital and had awarded purple hearts to forty wounded soldiers, including one dying man. This emotional scene was still raw in Patton's mind when he saw Kuhl.

The slapping incidents nearly ended Patton's career. Most likely, they cost Patton command of the American ground forces during Operation Overlord, the invasion of France in 1944. Eisenhower doubted Patton's emotional state because of the slappings. These came on top of Patton's long record of speaking inappropriately about fellow American and British generals and a host of other topics. Patton was removed from command of the Seventh Army, and Omar Bradley became commander of American forces during the Normandy invasion.

Patton eventually did receive command of the Third Army, which he led to glory across northern France and into Germany in 1944 and 1945.

Bradley felt Patton was a much different soldier in the summer of 1944 than he had been a year earlier, describing Patton as "a judicious, reasonable, and likeable commander." He attributed the change to the slapping incidents and claimed that Private Kuhl had done more than any other private in the army to win the war in Europe.

Carlo D'Este and others have a different outlook on how the war's outcome may have been altered by the sanctions Patton received for slapping Kuhl and Bennett. D'Este suggests that had Patton commanded all the American ground forces, he might have been more aggressive than Bradley was and decisively defeated the Germans west of the River Seine in Normandy, ending the war in autumn 1944 instead of May 1945. He also suggests the Battle of the Bulge would not have been as initially successful for the Germans if Patton had been army group commander. Patton might have paid better attention to the evidence pointing to a German offensive and then would have acted quicker than Bradley did once the Germans attacked.

General George S. Patton died in December 1945 from injuries suffered in an automobile accident in Luxembourg.

Charles Kuhl returned to the Mishawaka area and worked at Bendix. He died in Mishawaka on January 31, 1971, and is buried in Mishawaka's Fairview Cemetery.

Charles Kuhl is buried in Fairview Cemetery, Mishawaka.

CHAPTER 17

"WE DO OUR BEST AND HAVE FUN": COACH FRANCIS HILL AND THE FORGOTTEN 1948 AND 1949 MISHAWAKA HIGH SCHOOL CROSS COUNTRY TEAMS

In the late 1940s, Mishawaka High School's cross country program ranked among Indiana's elite. The 1946 Maroons, coached by Dutch Thurston, were co-champions with Anderson High School in the first-ever IHSAA state meet. Their state championship banner has hung in the Mishawaka gym for many years, along with other Cavemen championship and runner-up banners.

Nearly forgotten over the decades, though, were the 1948 and 1949 Mishawaka cross country teams, who finished just short of state championships. Coached by Francis Hill, both were runner-up to powerful teams from Anderson.

Francis Hill coached the Mishawaka High School cross country team to state runner-up finishes in 1948 and 1949.

1948

When Coach Thurston turned over the reins of the Mishawaka program after the 1947 season, the Maroon harriers had a state championship to their credit, a third-place finish in 1947, and twenty consecutive dual-meet wins.

Francis Hill kept Mishawaka cross country on a winning course in his first season in 1948. The Maroons finished 8-0, running their dual meet streak to 28 victories.

Going into the sectional at Mishawaka's Eberhart Golf Course, Hill's team was favored over top rivals Elkhart and LaPorte. The Maroons lived up to expectations, scoring 46 to LaPorte's 88 and Elkhart's 90. Using bursts of speed in the last hundred yards to overtake fatigued opponents, co-captains Don Wood and Lawrence Healy finished sixth and seventh to lead the balanced Mishawaka runners. Mishawaka took five of the top thirteen places, with Ed Partridge in ninth, Stan Ross in eleventh, and Bill Butts in thirteenth.

Don Wood emphasized the team concept as part of Mishawaka's success: "This team was more like a family than a team. The team was more important; one person doesn't cut it." The "big camaraderie" of the team carried over to the course: "We pretty much always ran in a group. During the meets we would chant" to encourage each other. This also had an intimidating effect on opponents. "It would shake them," Wood admitted.

Ross said Hill and Thurston taught a basic rule about running in a group: "You would never pass up one of your own runners and just blow by him. You'd always slow down and run with him because if you could pull him up, you could really improve your score...Everybody was significant." Hill and Thurston's strategy caused runners to push each other to keep up and usually placed several in the top ten in any meet.

After the 1948 season was completed, team members published a summary of the year. They wrote, "We have nearly always run in a group as long as possible. This way we encourage each other and discourage the other runners by talking to each other and yelling. We also found that we can keep each other more relaxed by running together."

Stan Ross remembered that some of their team spirit came from getting in a circle to do calisthenics: "Everyone yelled," while doing them. "It was a bonding thing." Following each victory in 1948, Mishawaka also continued its tradition of doing a yell for their opponents.

The Maroons' team concept extended off the cross country course, too. Ross noted that team manager Camiel DeMeester would often walk back to the high school during practices at Eberhart or Merrifield Park to get extra shoestrings or bandages, or anything else the team needed. The Maroon harriers also ate lunch together, and following the season, the boys organized the team banquet for their parents and coaches.

Ross explained that the Thurston and Hill teams combined discipline with fun: "Nobody cut corners...Whatever Coach said, we did...Thurston would seldom talk about winning. It was about fun. And if you didn't win, it wasn't as fun." Hill continued this approach, with the focus being, "We do our best and have fun," moreso than winning a state title.

Four days after the 1948 sectional, Mishawaka won the twenty-team Northern Indiana High School Conference Meet with 53 points to Fort Wayne North's 105. The Maroons placed five runners in the top 16.

Winning the conference made Mishawaka a title contender at the state meet in Indianapolis, but still underdogs to Anderson, looking for its third consecutive championship. First-year coach Hill shared his runners' nervousness about the big meet. "At the state meet, [Hill] was so nervous that we had to light his cigarette for him," remembered Stan Ross.

Sixteen teams competed at the state finals, held at Coffin Golf

Mishawaka High School took this team to the 1948 state finals meet: back: Coach Dutch Thurston, Stan Ross, Larry Healy, Ed Partridge, Bill Butts, Coach Francis Hill
front: Ralph Kaiser, Don Wood, John Stafford, Jim Lang, Camiel DeMeester

Stan Ross, an accomplished woodworker, created this plaque honoring his team's accomplishments.

Course in Indianapolis. Mishawaka continued its strategy of running in a pack. Ross recalled a photo of the Maroon runners together during the state meet: "I remember you could see a blob of gold and maroon." Anderson, though, was too much for Mishawaka, winning 56-73. Vincennes was third with 81. The team yearbook recorded, "Anderson's team ran an exceptionally good race and its best of the season...We did not run as well as we should have or the scoring would have been much closer."

After the season, the team also wrote, "Each of the seven boys running on our team received silver medals for winning second place in the State Championship Meet. This was a great honor for our school, our team, and ourselves. Our coach was very proud of us and we were very proud of him, for Mr. Hill had done a very fine job of guiding us throughout the season."

1949

Returning to the state finals in 1949 would prove an even greater challenge for Coach Hill and the cross country team after losing Wood, Healy, and seven other seniors off the 1948 squad. Despite their inexperience, Mishawaka's dominance continued as the Maroons went 9-0 in their dual meets.

A few days before the conference meet, Hill wrote Stan Ross and Larry Healy, then freshmen at Ball State, offering them an update on the team's progress and insight for us into the coach's thinking:

> *Their spirit is high, they have shown improvement in running form and ability to stay the distance...Our pace will have to improve to be title contenders.*
>
> *[At the conference meet] the one thing in our favor is the fact that the course is a very tough one, and barring injury or illness somebody will have to run like H--L to beat us. The outcome Sat. will, more or less, be in the lap of the gods.*
>
> *Regardless of the outcome, they have begun to catch the cross country spirit. Whether you know it or not, you fellows have been running with us in each meet and particularly last Thurs. [when Mishawaka won its 37th straight dual meet]. Likewise, you'll be with us Sat...There are still some things that need to be done in the way of mental attitude, team spirit, etc. but that will take time. Dutch seems to think they have been coming along very well and he is right, but I can't give in to the idea of running second to any body.*

As a tune-up for the sectional, Mishawaka won the NIHSC meet with 47 points against runner-up Hammond's 103. Consistency from Mishawaka's top runners helped the Maroons continue their supremacy, finishing with five of the top fourteen places.

Paul Williams, a senior who joined the team in 1949, recalled well Hill's strategy of running as a team. During races, he said, "We talked,

In 1949 the Mishawaka High School cross country team was again state runner-up.
back: Jim Stricker, Carl Hunt, Paul Williams, Tom Chamberlin
front: Bill Alberts, John Stafford, Ralph Powell

we hollered at each other," when running in a "wild pack" for the first mile and a half of the race. They also would talk about runners from other teams as the pack of Maroons passed them. Williams said they made comments like, "Look at that guy-- he's looking tired." He continued, "We just went out there and ran fun," but other teams ran as individuals in grim silence.

Hill's harriers also had fun off the cross country course. Williams explains that the team usually drove to meets in several cars, including the car Hill used for his driver's ed classes. John Stafford would always sit up front, and Coach Hill allowed him to rev the engine after victories, using the vehicle's dual controls. "When you're winning, you can do that," Williams added, smiling.

Mishawaka entered the sectional at Eberhart as heavy favorites and scored 34, well ahead of LaPorte's 78 and Central's 89. Mishawaka did not have the individual champion, but Williams, Jim Stricker, John Stafford, Ralph Powell, and Charles Albert, in the fourth through ninth positions, gave Hill's team a winning balance.

The week before state, Hill ran the cross country team eight miles a night, recalled Paul Williams. "We went around that place [Merrifield] so many times it made you dizzy. [Hill] was trying to psyche us up to win one more for him."

Again strong challengers, Mishawaka returned to the state finals, trying to depose the Anderson Indians. Mishawaka faced some unexpected obstacles at the state meet. Jim Stricker was sick with the flu the week before the state finals. Also, Anderson's runners dressed in different-colored uniforms to make it more difficult for Mishawaka to know whom to pass. Hill considered these problems, and, according to Williams, advised his team, "Just go out and run hard.'"

Anderson came away with a 67-79 win, but in a closer contest than in 1948. Vincennes placed a distant third with 125. Had just one Mishawaka runner been three seconds faster, the Maroons would have been state champions. The ill Stricker finished in a pack twenty seconds behind where he would normally have been.

This was Mishawaka's only loss in 1949, and despite some natural disappointment at the narrow defeat, Paul Williams remembered, "Nobody was sitting around with their heads low. Second place was pretty good...It was a fun year. We whipped everybody but Anderson."

Perspectives

Francis Hill continued coaching the Mishawaka cross country team with great success for two more seasons, but never again would Mishawaka be as dominant as in 1948 and 1949. In 1950 the Maroons went 7-2, running the consecutive winning streak to 42 before a loss to rival LaPorte. A second place at the NIHSC meet and a sectional title were followed by a sixth place at the state meet, where Ralph Powell was third. Mishawaka went 8-3 in 1951 and finished sixteenth in the state.

What was the secret to the success of the Hill and Thurston cross country teams?

Don Wood suggested some of their success may have resulted from giving each runner a tablespoon of "caratal," a sugar mix, before each meet "to give you a quick burst of energy." He added with a laugh, "They probably wouldn't let you do that today."

Powell gave his insight on the teams' work ethic: "There's no question in my mind that we dominated because we worked harder and had the strength." Hill's teams were ahead of their time in using aerobic workouts: "We worked really hard on calisthenics, which gave us strength and explosiveness."

The demanding practices included laps at both the Merrifield Park course and the steep hills at Eberhart near the Virgil Street pumping station. Wood recalled, "We did spend an awful lot of time running around the waterworks hill...until you felt like you wanted to bury yourself," but all the hill running paid off, he adds.

Paul Williams said, "[Hill] convinced us that nobody could run hills like we could. So when we came to a course with hills, we'd just eat it up...We'd probably run as much psychological as physical...If he said we could do it, we believed it." He noted that Hill taught them to take short steps up the hills, and that, along with endurance, was decisive.

Ralph Powell attributed the success of Hill's teams to great conditioning and having a team-oriented attitude: "All runners have pains. Being in a group, it was a little easier to run through them...We took great pride in running beyond that discomfort barrier."

One story from Powell's senior season, in 1950, illustrates what he believed to be the superior "volume and intensity" of Hill's conditioning regimen. The week before the state meet, runners from South Bend Central suggested they and Mishawaka work out together. At that point, unlike 1949, the Maroons were winding down their workouts, doing perhaps only half of a regular season practice. Nonetheless, Powell recalled the Central runners saying, "It was the hardest workout we had all year.'"

Williams echoed the team sentiments of other Hill runners: "He taught us a lot more than about how to run up hills...He taught us to be a group. Maybe that was one of the things that rubbed off. Going to meets, we hardly ever talked, but coming back we were like a bunch of magpies."

Stan Ross, Milt Ross, Ralph Powell, and several other Hill runners became teachers and coaches, influenced in part by their experience in cross country. Stan Ross explained, "Seniors and juniors would help coach the freshmen." He remembered looking at a group of freshmen and thinking that in that group there might have been only one or two great runners, but he was impressed with how hard they worked: "I thought, if kids want to try that hard, I want to teach and coach." As a result, he switched his intended major from engineering to teaching.

Francis Hill resigned as cross country coach after the 1951 season and continued teaching at Mishawaka until before his death in 1970. His career dual meet record of 32-5 is one of the highest winning per-

In February 1998 members of the the Hill-era cross country teams returned to Mishawaka High School for a reunion and the presentation of their long-overdue state runner-up banners.
back: Murphy Rafferty, Keith Miller, Ralph Powell, Paul Williams, Neil Tracy, John Magrames, Milt Ross, Cloyd Partridge, Jim Haughee
front: Stan Ross, Camiel DeMeester, Jim Lang, Jim Stricker, Don Wood, Jack Davis, Harry Larrimore, Chuck Golba

The cross country alumni proudly display their state runner-up banners and receive a standing ovation from the crowd at the Mishawaka-Northridge basketball game.

centages (87%) of any coach in MHS history. Hill's teams won 22 consecutive dual meets, two conference titles, and three sectionals, along with two state runner-up finishes.

Despite all this success, Mishawaka High School overlooked Hill's runner-up teams when banners were created in the early 1980s to honor Cavemen state championship and runner-up teams. This omission was finally corrected on February 7, 1998, when two new banners for these unheralded runner-up teams were presented to hang with those for other great Mishawaka teams, including the 1946 cross country state champions. The ceremony held at halftime of the Mishawaka-Northridge basketball game also introduced members of the 1948 and 1949 teams, who were given a standing ovation they had waited half a century for.

Long overlooked, the Mishawaka cross country teams of the late 1940s wrote an important chapter in one of the richest high school athletic traditions in northern Indiana. In the years since those great teams, Mishawaka has continued as an area power in cross country, following the course set over fifty years ago by the Thurston and Hill teams.

Decades after the last Maroon crossed the finish line at the 1948 and 1949 state meets, their teams' banners finally hang at Mishawaka High School, honoring past greatness and inspiring future achievements.

CHAPTER 18

REMEMBERING ROBERT F. KENNEDY'S VISIT TO MISHAWAKA

Mentioning the spring of 1968 causes most Americans to think of two events: the assassinations of Martin Luther King in April and Robert Kennedy in June.

Mishawakans old enough to remember that tumultuous spring also recall Robert Kennedy's campaign appearance in Mishawaka. In fact, in the weeks before the May Indiana Democratic primary, three presidential candidates focused on winning the Democratic vote in the Princess City.

In 1968 Indiana was the stage for a great political drama. Minnesota senator Eugene McCarthy had been the first to announce that he would challenge President Lyndon Johnson for the 1968 Democratic nomination. New York senator Robert Kennedy had been reluctant to run against an incumbent president of his own party, but he shared McCarthy's opposition to Johnson's Vietnam War policy.

Prior to McCarthy's stunning victory over Johnson in the March 12 New Hampshire primary, Kennedy had begun to seriously consider entering the presidential race. The January 1968 Tet Offensive by the Vietnamese communists and the silence with which Johnson received the recommendations of the Kerner Commission on urban violence, both influenced Kennedy to announce his candidacy on March 16.

The Kennedy campaign's first major test was whether to enter the Indiana primary, the first primary still open for Kennedy. Indiana provided a true challenge for Kennedy. He would have to defeat McCarthy and Indiana governor Roger Branigin, a favorite-son stand-in for President Johnson and, later, Vice-President Hubert Humphrey, who had declared his candidacy that spring after Johnson bowed out. Branigin had the support of the state's Democratic organization, and Kennedy faced an uphill battle in Indiana as a liberal Easterner and an outspoken critic of the war.

Nevertheless, Kennedy hoped Indiana would provide him with a victory like West Virginia had for his brother in 1960, propelling him to the nomination and the White House.

In the month before the May 7 primary, Robert Kennedy focused much of his campaigning and perhaps $2-3 million on winning Indiana. He visited St. Joseph County four times, including a May 2 rally in downtown Mishawaka.

On May 1 Kennedy's campaign announced that he would appear in Mishawaka, while traveling from South Bend to Elkhart and back. Initially, a downtown rally was planned, with a stop at the Town and Country Shopping Center, while returning from Elkhart.

Rally sites like these were favorites of the Kennedy campaign. For little expense, the candidate could generate the appearance of an enthusiastic throng of supporters. Likewise, Kennedy used the motorcade to greet and be seen by thousands of people.

Prior to the Kennedy appearance in Mishawaka, both McCarthy and Branigin had made campaign stops in the Princess City. Branigin had visited the Kosciuszko Club on April 26, and McCarthy's rally had drawn several hundred supporters on April 27.

By Thursday, May 2, Kennedy's plans for visiting Mishawaka had changed. The Town and Country stop had been dropped in favor of a longer downtown rally in front of the First National Bank at Lincoln Way and Main Street.

Although Kennedy was an hour late for his 6:30 PM appearance in downtown Mishawaka, the several thousand supporters and on-look-

Senator Robert F. Kennedy is surrounded by a crowd of thousands in down-
town Mishawaka on May 2, 1968. Scenes like this were common during the
Kennedy campaign that spring. Kennedy was greeted like a celebrity, not
just a political candidate.

Kennedy spoke to the crowd of thousands from this platform on South Main
Street near the First National Bank.

ers were still enthusiastic. The **South Bend Tribune** described the huge crowd at the Four Corners as one of the largest political gatherings in Mishawaka history, and none has surpassed it since.

In addition to local Democratic officials, the Kennedy entourage in Mishawaka included his wife Ethel, who usually accompanied the candidate during the campaign, and former St. Louis Cardinals star Stan Musial.

Kennedy's comments to the Mishawaka crowd echoed ideas he stated throughout the Hoosier campaign. The candidate was careful to tone down his liberal ideas to appeal to the more conservative Indiana electorate. He proclaimed his opposition to urban and campus rioting, but noted, too, that he wanted to end the educational and employment discrimination that led to rioting. Kennedy also tried to allay fears about his stand on Vietnam by saying he opposed unilateral American withdrawal from Vietnam. Instead, the South Vietnamese would need to take on a greater share of their own defense. He expressed belief in negotiation, but reminded the crowd that he would be tough on communism, as the Kennedy Administration had been during the 1962 Cuban Missile Crisis.

The **Tribune** reported that the heaviest crowds for the Kennedy motorcade were from downtown Mishawaka to downtown South Bend. The route went down Eighth Street and Milburn Boulevard, through Mishawaka's ethnic and heavily Democratic West End. The Kennedy campaign drew substantial support from ethnic whites, African Americans, and Hispanics, and sought out opportunities to have the senator be with those groups. Many waited in parked cars, on porches, or along curbs for the senator to drive by. Kennedy shook hands all along the route taken by his slow-moving convertible.

That evening thousands of Mishawakans must have seen Kennedy, either at the downtown rally or along his motorcade route. Hundreds shook Kennedy's hand or at least made physical contact with him. Merle Blue, then a social studies teacher at Mishawaka High School, recalls asking his students the next day how many actually touched the senator. A large number of Blue's students raised their hands.

Two incidents from Robert Kennedy's visit to Mishawaka illustrate the intensity of crowds during his campaign. As he pulled up to the rally site in downtown Mishawaka, so many people were pushing against his car that two small children were in danger of being crushed. Robert and Ethel Kennedy pulled the children into the car to prevent their injury.

Along the motorcade route, one handshake that lasted too long pulled Kennedy from his moving car, and he fell to the street. He climbed back in, and the motorcade resumed its route, with Kennedy continuing to shake hands. This type of accident happened on other occasions, too, during Kennedy's campaign that spring.

Although the senator cut his lip when he fell, Kennedy aides denied reports that he chipped a tooth. However, in **85 Days**, Jules Witcover, a reporter who covered Kennedy throughout the campaign, says Kennedy did chip a tooth in his fall and soon had it capped.

Robert Kennedy's intense campaigning in Indiana and his stop in Mishawaka paid off well on election day. He won 42% of the Indiana Democratic vote, compared to 31% for Branigin and 27% for McCarthy. Kennedy, despite efforts to portray himself as the under-dog, enjoyed broad support throughout the state, winning 10 of 11 congressional districts and 57 of 92 counties. Indiana's 63 convention delegates were Kennedy's, at least for the first ballot.

Kennedy's win was even more impressive in Mishawaka. He won all five districts, 26 of 31 precincts, and was second in the five precincts he did not win. Kennedy had over 50% of the Mishawaka Democratic vote, compared to McCarthy's 29.4% and Branigin's 20.4%. Kennedy's biggest margins of victory came in precincts that voted at the BK Club and D'Amici's Club in the West End.

The Kennedy victory was solid throughout St. Joseph County, as he captured 48% of the Democratic vote and all six districts in South Bend. McCarthy was a distant second in the county with 32%.

In Indiana Kennedy had shown the Democratic Party that his base of support extended beyond his "have-not coalition" of blacks and eth-nic whites. He knew he would need to send that message in a conven-tion show-down with McCarthy or Humphrey.

Robert Kennedy went on to victories in Nebraska and Washington,

DC, before losing in Oregon. On June 4, he convincingly won the South Dakota and California primaries, which positioned him well for the convention. Just past midnight on June 5, after declaring victory in California, Kennedy was shot in Los Angeles. He died from his wounds early on the morning of June 6.

Hubert Humphrey went on to receive the Democratic presidential nomination at the infamous, strife-ridden convention in Chicago. Humphrey, burdened by the convention debacle and the administration's Vietnam and domestic policies, narrowly lost to Richard Nixon in the November election.

CHAPTER 19

YEAR OF THE KINGSMEN: PENN HIGH SCHOOL'S 1999 ACADEMIC STATE CHAMPIONSHIPS

During the 1990s Penn High School's enrollment grew from 2100 students to over 2900. At the same time, the school's accomplishments in interscholastic competition increased even more impressively. Kingsmen athletes brought home eight team state titles and numerous conference and post-season honors. Earning greater success, though, were Penn's academic teams, which won nine state championships between 1992 and 1999.

Prior to the mid-1980s, Penn students wanting to participate on an academic team had only speech and debate to choose from. Soon, though, new academic competitions proliferated, presenting many options for bright students who wanted to challenge themselves and represent their school. Penn High School made a strong commitment to achieving excellence in these new academic events.

A decade of achievement in academic competition for Penn reached its climax in 1999 as the Quiz Bowl, social studies, and Spell Bowl teams all returned home with the ultimate prize: a state championship.

Quiz Bowl

During the 1990s, the Penn Quiz Bowl team advanced four times to the championship match of the St. Joseph Valley League tourney, only to lose to its nemesis, St. Joseph's High School. The painful Kingsmen losses came in 1991, 1993, 1997, and 1998. The 1997 and 1998 Penn teams had won regular season league championships with victories over the Indians, only to be turned back at tourney time. Particularly agonizing to the Kingsmen faithful was the 365-360 finals loss in 1997. In 1992 and 1996, Penn had also advanced to the semi-finals of the league tourney, meeting with defeat by Adams and Mishawaka, respectively.

Despite the local post-season disappointments, with the advent of the Quiz Bowl state tourney in 1997, Penn had been able to achieve success down-state. The Kingsmen tied for third in the inaugural state finals, and were runner-up behind Andrean in 1998.

Penn had established itself as one of the state's most powerful Quiz Bowl programs, but also as a team that seemed unable to win a tournament championship.

This would change in 1999.

At the start of the 1998-99 campaign, Penn Quiz Bowl coach Susan Van Fleit had some rebuilding to do, but returned a solid nucleus from the 15-3 state runner-up team. Mainstays Jake Brenner and Andrew Reed would be difficult to replace, but seniors Mason O'Dell and Alex Tawadros had been major contributors throughout the previous season. "We knew our two seniors were going to carry us-- Alex and Mason-- and they did," observed Van Fleit. Joining them would be senior Jason Ridenour and juniors Aaron Rosenfeld and Nathan Meng. Throughout the 1998-99 season, other students would see some varsity playing time, but these five would lead the Kingsmen through the league schedule and into post-season play.

The local Quiz Bowl season ran from November to February, with the state finals at the end of April. Penn began practices in October. Coach Van Fleit shared her practice regimen and philosophy: "We practice three times a week about a month before the season actually begins. Then we practice twice a week, and we have the match on the third day. I have been surprised to find out that that's actually more practice than many of the other schools do...I like to try to make the practices resemble matches as closely as possible...We practice in order to build confidence, to build speed. But as far as actually learning material, they have to do a lot of that on their own...They can pick up a lot at practice, but I think working on speed, working together, is almost more important to try to develop during a practice."

Nathan Meng agreed: "The most effective preparation was not as much studying the material as it was speed work. During our long season, we constantly worked on speed and accuracy to carry us the distance."

Mason O'Dell valued practices for building team cohesiveness: "Probably the most effective preparation for the team was just hanging around each other. Everyone was able to joke around at any time and this helped us stay loose during competitions."

While preparing for the 1998-99 season, the Kingsmen were thinking about the goal of winning the league season and tourney championships and making another state title run. They also were dealing with the fall-out from a scandal that shook the St. Joseph Valley Quiz Bowl League at the end of the 1998 season.

After the league championship match, St. Joe coach Ben Dillon had admitted that for years his teams had been reviewing videotapes of previous years' tourney matches to better prepare themselves for post-season questions. Dillon and the Indians saw nothing wrong with this tactic, which was not forbidden by league rules. Other schools, though, were incensed by what they saw as cheating. Clay and Penn, who had lost in the tourney to St. Joe more than any other schools had, thought about how many titles they might have won during St. Joe's decade of domination, had Dillon not resorted to the videotapes.

After much protesting, the end result was that St. Joe kept its tainted championships, and the league got new questions for use in future years to prevent anyone else from gaining an advantage through videotapes. League administrators had done their best to bury the controversy, but many in the league were left with an aftertaste of resentment.

While the Kingsmen were thinking of what might have been in

those four finals losses, they could also begin the new season knowing that St. Joe would be minus its video advantage come tourney time, making a fair playing field for all.

Penn opened the season with a decisive win over Adams, 320-185, followed by a narrower triumph against Clay, 285-210. Beating the Colonials avenged the only loss the Kingsmen suffered during the 1997-98 regular season.

The Penn juggernaut picked up momentum by pounding Elkhart Central, 365-120, and LaSalle, 485-270. Van Fleit recalled, "As we started the season and we did so well every week, I started thinking this might just be it."

Wins against crosstown rivals Marian, 270-175, and Mishawaka, 325-185, followed. New Prairie became the next Penn victim, 305-150, as the Kingsmen stood alone atop the league.

Thinking about being undefeated and in first place and looking ahead to the showdown with St. Joe the following week, may have contributed to the Kingsmen's biggest scare of the regular season. Against Riley, Penn trailed late in the match, but rescued a 210-180 decision to remain perfect.

The St. Joe Indians came to Penn, and in an emotionally charged match, were thoroughly outclassed by the Kingsmen, 385-190. This was the largest margin of victory Penn had ever posted against St. Joe.

Penn ended its scorched-earth campaign through the league schedule the following week with a 325-195 pasting of Washington. Beating the Panthers completed the first undefeated regular season in Penn Quiz Bowl history. Coach Van Fleit explained what this achievement meant: "Just the fact that we were undefeated during the season was really exciting. Even if we hadn't won the state tournament, that would have been a major high point in my years of coaching, because to go undefeated a whole season really is not easy. So that was great."

Penn entered the 1999 league tourney as the favorite, despite the history of St. Joe victories in the post-season. Van Fleit's charges had outscored their regular season opponents 3275-1860, an average margin of victory of 141 points per match.

Earning a first-round bye in the tourney, Penn opened the post-season by smothering Washington, 290-115, in the best defensive effort of the year.

This set up the tourney semi-finals and finals, held at the WNDU-TV studios on Saturday evening, February 27. Penn and St. Joseph's were paired in the first semi-final, followed by Marian and Adams. It seemed to most that the first semi-final would be the **de facto** championship match, with neither Marian or Adams having the firepower needed to down the Kingsmen or Indians.

Against St. Joe, Penn trailed at the end of the first toss-up round, 55-30. The Kingsmen then used an offensive assault in the toss-up and bonus round, outscoring the stunned Indians 90-15 to open a 120-70 lead.

The defending champions whittled away at this margin in the 60-second round, trailing 180-160 going into the fourth round. The Indians actually outscored Penn 55-50 in the final round of toss-up, as the Kingsmen offense struggled to get just three questions correct. Penn took a 230-215 lead into the dramatic final question. St. Joe buzzed in first on the 15-point question, desperately hoping to force the overtime round. They missed, though, and the Penn celebration started.

While Penn had beaten St. Joe four times in the 1990s during the regular season, they had never bested St. Joe head-to-head in a tournament. The Kingsmen victory emphatically ended an eleven-year Indian streak of league tourney titles.

The win over St. Joe understandably stood out in Penn team members' thoughts. According to O'Dell, "Being able to prove that we were the superior team after what happened the year before was one of the most rewarding moments of my life." Aaron Rosenfeld recalled, "Beating St. Joe was particularly satisfying. Having never beaten them made it all the sweeter when it came down to the last question and we won." To Meng the win was a "defining moment" that showed Penn had "ended St. Joe's dominance."

The match against Adams later that evening felt more like an after-thought than a title contest. Even the Eagles seemed to go into the match resigned to an inevitable defeat. Penn took an early lead and cruised the rest of the way to the 340-210 championship victory. For over a decade, Penn had hunted the league tourney title, and finally it was theirs. "When we won the league tournament, then I really knew we were on the way to good things," Susan Van Fleit reflected.

The champs had an eight-week layover before the April 24 state finals at Brownsburg High School. With a 13-0 record, Penn would go down state as a favorite, with undefeated Andrean a solid contender for a repeat title. Sixteen schools from four academic conferences were at the state finals. Clay, Marian, and St. Joe joined Penn as representatives from the St. Joseph Valley League. In 1999 fifty-three schools participated in the leagues that sent their best to Brownsburg.

Going into the state finals, Van Fleit was optimistic about Penn's chances: "We had been in the state finals before. We were confident. We were just on a roll. It just all worked out. And we were relaxed. I wasn't really nervous. It just seemed like it was going to happen. They had proven themselves. It wasn't a surprise."

The 1999 Penn Quiz Bowl team is shown here in a preliminary-round match at the state finals, held at Brownsburg High School.

The Kingsmen knew how to stay relaxed, here playing a round of euchre before the state championship match against Andrean.

In the three morning preliminary rounds, Penn downed Shelbyville 295-135, Perry Meridian 285-180, and Cardinal Ritter 265-185. While the first two matches were not close, Penn trailed Ritter 170-140 going into the final round. The veteran Penn team stepped up to the challenge and proceeded to crush the Raiders by outscoring them 125-15 in the last round to get the win.

Penn, 1997 state champ Center Grove, and defending champion Andrean each took 3-0 records into the afternoon semi-finals and were joined by Blackford with one loss.

In a rematch of 1998's state semi-final match, Penn faced Center Grove and put on an impressive offensive and defensive display. The Kingsmen outscored the Trojans 90-25 in the first round and 90-0 in the second round. Before Center Grove knew what hit them, it was over, 355-185.

During the afternoon matches, Penn's composure and state finals experience began to show their effects. After dismantling Center

Grove, the Penn students returned to the euchre game they had been playing during much of the lunch break. Meng explained, "Our team was mentally fresh at the state tournament. Instead of studying in between matches like other teams, we rested and took our minds out of our 'situation' by playing cards. In doing so, our team was more focused and less stressed." Rosenfeld added, "This helped us to maintain our level-headedness."

The victory over Center Grove set up a rematch of the 1998 title contest, Penn vs. Andrean. The 1999 final was a clash of academic titans, both undefeated on the season. The 59ers held a scant 40-35 lead after the first round, but the Kingsmen evened the score at 55 by the end of the second round. In the 60-second round, Penn opened a 145-125 margin and refused to relinquish it.

Going into the final question of the match, Penn held a fifteen point

Penn High School, 1999 Quiz Bowl state champions
back: Assistant Coach Les Kistler, Jason Ridenour, Nathan Meng
front: Aaron Rosenfeld, Mason O'Dell, Alex Tawadros, Coach Susan Van Fleit

advantage, 195-180. In a repeat of the league tourney semi-final with St. Joe, Andrean buzzed in first, seeking a correct answer that would have tied the match and sent it into sudden death. They missed, sealing the state championship for Penn.

Van Fleit described her thoughts during the Andrean match: "I think my confidence kind of went up and down during that last match...I just did feel that they would do it. They were on. All of them were in sync...Everyone contributed. It wasn't one person just taking over, which usually doesn't work...They just jelled at that point, and we could count on all of them for various reasons. Nobody had a down day, lucky for us. We were thrilled to have won...They did really the best job they could possibly do because they were all just coming up with answers that I found unbelievable."

The Kingsmen had finished the season an incredible 18-0, winning every title they sought in 1999.

Penn had produced other outstanding Quiz Bowl teams, but what made the 1999 team a state champion? According to Susan Van Fleit, "It was a combination of several factors. First of all, you have to have students with a good background in academics...They usually have good memories; they retained a lot. They do a lot of reading. So that's what they bring to the team, and that's what we had on that team. We also need kids who enjoy the play and enjoy the process...We had a group that really enjoyed it. They liked winning. They were competitive; sometimes they were a little bit too competitive with each other, but it worked for them that year. They were confident...It was all those factors that just came together."

The 1999 Quiz Bowl championship also reflected the strength of the Penn academic competitions program. The Quiz Bowl team's success had contributed to and resulted from the excellence being expected of Penn academic competitors as a whole. Van Fleit appreciated this relationship: "I just feel very pleased, very happy to be in a system where academic competition is valued...That whole environment fosters our success with lots of academic teams. It's not just the strange few kids who compete in academics. There are a lot of kids and a lot of adults around here who value what they do, and I'm not sure that's true in every school. That is a big factor in our success."

A year later, the state title had only grown in value for members of the Penn Quiz Bowl team. "It's an honor to be a member of a state championship team. At first, I did not realize the impact of what being a state champion felt like. I thought it was just another common thing. Yet, after a prolonged period of rest after the championship, I believe that it bolstered my confidence not only in my studies but in myself, that I could rely on what I thought and not worry if what I thought was wrong," expressed Nathan Meng.

Aaron Rosenfeld saw the championship as "a great honor that no one can take away from me. It is my one brief moment to stand in the sun and feel a sense of self-dignity that will stay with me the rest of my life."

Coach Van Fleit believed the 1999 championship also elevated the expectations she had for the program and future Quiz Bowl teams: "It kind of makes you hungrier once you were able to do it, to get the championship. So now I'm thinking this is a real goal that we need to keep our eyes on from the beginning and keep those kids thinking this is possible, this is something we need to work toward. If we had never won a championship, I'm not so sure that I would think quite that way. Once you've won it, you realize that really is a goal that is attainable."

After a decade of impressive accomplishments and some painful losses, the Penn Quiz Bowl program achieved its ultimate goal. The 1999 state championship was also shared, in spirit, by dozens of the school's Quiz Bowl alumni who had also sought league or state titles, only to fall short. Penn's state championship Quiz Bowl trophy would stand as a monument to persistence, faith, and commitment to excellence. It also pointed the way toward more great things for the Kingsmen in 1999.

Academic Super Bowl Social Studies

Academic Super Bowl social studies is played in 299 high schools in Indiana.

And then there is Penn.

In the latter half of the 1990s, few teams dominated any competition in Indiana like Penn High School did in Academic Super Bowl social studies. Winning state titles with undefeated teams in 1996 and 1997 and placing eleventh in the state in 1998, Penn amassed a 230-29-1 record (.887) in seven seasons. In 1999 the Kingsmen returned the entire 1998 team, six players who had been undefeated through the regular season and the regional before losing in the state finals. Penn would be the team to beat in 1999.

Returning for Penn were senior captain Mason O'Dell, seniors John Peterson and Jason Ridenour, juniors Mike Vander Heyden and Trent McNeer, and sophomore Michelle Werts. Joining the team for the 1999 campaign were sophomore Laura Pajot and freshman Kyle Fisher. The team was coached by Pete De Kever.

Academic Super Bowl is a research-based competition in which students compete in five subject areas (math, English, fine arts, science, social studies) and an interdisciplinary round. Each subject area has its own team, with occasionally a few students competing on more than one team. Teams usually have four to eight members, with three students being able to participate in a competition at one time. Competitions consist of a round of 25 multiple choice questions. Students have twenty seconds to confer on the correct response, to be determined by the captain.

Each year, Indiana Academic Competitions for Excellence, sponsored by the Indiana Association of School Principals, chooses a broad theme for all the Academic Super Bowl subject areas. In 1999 the theme was "The Age of Enlightenment: 1650-1800." Each subject area was then given a study guide of topics and sources that questions would be based on.

The social studies outline in 1999 included the ideas of Adam Smith, Thomas Malthus, Thomas Hobbes, John Locke, Voltaire, Jean Jacques Rousseau, Thomas Jefferson, and Thomas Paine, mercantilism vs. free trade, divine right vs. constitutional monarchy, and documents of American democracy, such as the Declaration of Independence and the Constitution.

The hallmarks of the Penn social studies tradition of success have been getting some of Penn's best students on the team, starting preparation in early September, weeks or months before most teams, and investing many long hours of practice in the eight months that follow. In the first semester of the 1998-99 season, Penn practiced once a week for an hour and fifteen minutes. Preparation intensified in the second semester with two-a-week practices after school and three-hour practices on most weekends. Students invested almost 100 hours in practices during the season, with many more hours of reading and preparation on their own.

Penn players noted the importance of their practices. In an interview with WSBT-TV shortly after the season, Michelle Werts explained, "We have our three-hour practices on Sunday. I come out exhausted...because you study so hard and you go over everything. And you work for what you get." Eight months later she reflected, "Review was key to our success. It's one thing to know the information and go over it once. It is another to beat it into the ground. It was our dedication that brought us success."

"The most effective preparation for any team, especially ours, was to start early in the year. At the end of the year, we create our own games like Jeopardy, Trivial Pursuit, etc. to test each other's knowledge of the subject. This is successful since we are challenging ourselves, as well as the team," observed Trent McNeer.

"The practices help form a cohesive bond between team members. It helped make us know each other's strengths and weaknesses," stated John Peterson.

Kyle Fisher added, "The most effective preparation was the constant quizzing over material. As soon as the team thought they were done, there was new stuff to be reintroduced time and time again. The best thing was to just have it pounded into our heads over and over."

After six months of practice and preparation, the social studies team eagerly awaited its first competition, the Warsaw Invitational, on March 11. While the Kingsmen missed the first question of the meet, they exploded to answer correctly the next twelve, building a one-point advantage over Bethany Christian by question 13. Missing questions 14 and 17, Penn was still able to retain its narrow lead, 14-13, over Wawasee. The Kingsmen then put together a run, answering correctly six of the last seven questions, enough to win 21-18 over Bethany Christian and Wawasee.

Defeating the field of eleven other teams was a promising start to the season. According to Mike Vander Heyden, "Winning the season-opener was a great experience. Since our defeat at state the previous year, we needed to start the season off with a win and we did." McNeer echoed this sentiment, referring to Warsaw as "our first chance for redemption from our previous embarrassing defeat at state."

Things would not go so well for Penn the following week at the Duneland Conference Meet at Valparaiso. This was a competition, though, that the social studies team had dominated for the previous five years that Penn had competed there, winning first place each time. Penn also brought to the 1999 Duneland Meet a streak of eight consecutive championships at invitationals, stretching back to the 1995 Duneland Meet.

The Duneland Conference ran abbreviated Academic Super Bowl rounds of just twenty questions, in an effort to speed up an inevitably long evening. This made the round more of a sprint, giving less opportunity for a team that fell behind to catch up.

The social studies round began well for Penn, with the first five correct, before missing questions 6, 8, and 10. Despite this weak performance, Penn was tied with Michigan City at 7 by question 10. After both getting the next three right, the Kingsmen and Wolves remained deadlocked at 10. Penn trailed by one after missing 14 and then scored the next four questions correctly, but the solid Michigan City team dueled Penn point for point to maintain a slim advantage. Uncharacteristically, the Kingsmen faltered badly at the end of the round, missing two questions about the Declararation of Independence. Penn's errors in the final questions cost them not only a chance at the victory, but also allowed Andrean to capture second on a tiebreaker. Michigan City finished with 16 to Andrean and Penn's 14. It was the worst loss Penn had ever suffered in an invitational, and the Kingsmen's record stood at 20-2.

The loss to Michigan City and Andrean deeply disappointed Penn and called into question the team's preparation and chances for winning a state championship. Immediately after the round, though, team

Laura Pajot leads the Academic Super Bowl social studies team in a final review before the 1999 regional at LaPorte High School.

members began to analyze what went wrong, why questions were missed, and what topics would need extra review in the month remaining before the LaPorte regional.

"Valpo Invitational was a...definitive moment. Our loss to Michigan City and Andrean gave us a drive to study harder and wreak havoc when we had a rematch at regionals. We had revenge on the brain," recalled Werts.

Rather than getting down or placing blame, the Kingsmen positively converted their frustration, as Pajot described, "That was what kept us from becoming complacent and motivated us to work harder and review more on our own." Mason O'Dell agreed: "Everyone worked twice as hard to make sure nothing like this happened again."

Penn would have its chance at revenge soon enough at the regional on April 20. Although they missed questions 3 and 5 and trailed early, by question 10 the Kingsmen rallied to build a comfortable lead, 8-6, over Michigan City, Valparaiso, and Mishawaka.

In a round of tough questions, Penn missed two of the next five but clung to a two-point lead over Michigan City and Valparaiso through question 15.

The Kingsmen then stepped up their intensity when it was needed most, answering correctly eight of the last ten questions, to defeat the Wolves, 19-17. Penn, now 28-2, had won its fourth consecutive regional championship, sweetened by the taste of revenge for the March 18 disappointment. The loss was devastating to Michigan City. Having enjoyed its first victory over the Kingsmen, they expected to take the regional crown as well and qualify for the state finals, a feat no social studies team from the LaPorte regional, except Penn, had been able to do for at least seven years. As it turned out, Penn's regional score was high enough to qualify for the state finals, while the Wolves missed the cut-off by just a point.

"The regional was a 'statement' that Penn's previous loss was a fluke, and we backed it up by blowing away the competition. That was the most satisfying point in the season, since our confidence was still shaken from previous losses," remembered McNeer.

The Academic Super Bowl state finals were held on May 1, 1999, six years to the day that Penn first took a social studies team to the state finals. For the third year, the state finals were at Indianapolis Pike High School, a building with bittersweet memories for the Kingsmen social studies team. In 1997 Penn had dramatically won the state championship there on the last two questions, but in 1998, Penn had stumbled badly, finishing five points behind state champion Center Grove. The veterans of the 1998 team especially hoped that their championship quest would end more favorably with this trip to the Pike High School Performing Arts Center.

Captain Mason O'Dell, Laura Pajot, and John Peterson competed for Penn during the first ten questions of the championship round. The Kingsmen caught fire early and scored the first nine correct, finally being tripped up by a question about Malthus' belief in checking population growth. At the question 10 break, Penn, Delphi, and Elkhart Baptist were tied at 9, with six other schools just a point back.

Michelle Werts substituted in for Peterson, and Penn led Elkhart

Baptist and Greencastle, 14-13, through fifteen questions. "I remember that at about question 15, I knew the championship was ours. No matter what question it was, we were prepared for it," observed O'Dell.

The Kingsmen also correctly answered 16 before missing a question that asked for the author who first used the term "enlightened despot," Frederick the Great.

Penn would miss no more.

After question 20 Greencastle was tied with Penn at 18, a deadlock that remained through question 22. The decisive question of the round was 23, asking for the author of the quote, "The most formidable weapon against errors of every kind is reason." Penn correctly answered Thomas Paine, while the Tiger Cubs missed, dropping them back by one point, a margin they were unable to make up.

Gaining a lead-- no matter how small-- late in the state finals is thrilling, according to Werts: " I remember the excitement of sitting up on stage and slowly pulling away from the rest of the competitors and realizing that we were going to win."

The Kingsmen were by no means out of the woods yet, not with a scant one-point lead and two questions remaining. Because Academic Super Bowl tie-breaker rules emphasize performance in the final five questions, a team that loses a lead in the final questions will likely also lose the tiebreakers. Greencastle could not be counted on to miss, so Penn players knew they had to remain perfect through the end.

In question 24 Penn correctly associated Milton Friedman with laissez-faire economics, but Greencastle also got this right.

The entire competition and the state championship hung on question 25, which asked how the British constitution differed most radically from the American Constitution. The Kingsmen knew that the biggest difference was that the British constitution was unwritten. Greencastle also answered correctly, but Penn had held its narrow lead, defeating stubborn Greencastle 23-22, with West Lafayette and Elkhart Baptist a distant third at 20.

"While we were sitting on stage and waiting to leave as the champions, it was so surreal but yet really calm. It was such a great experience," recalled Michelle Werts.

Penn High School, 1999 Academic Super Bowl social studies state champions back: John Peterson, Captain Mason O'Dell, Jason Ridenour front: Coach Pete De Kever, Kyle Fisher, Laura Pajot, Michelle Werts, Trent McNeer not pictured: Mike Vander Heyden

Trent McNeer was thinking of the 1997 and 1998 state finals after question 25: "My first thoughts after we had clinched the title was that Penn was back. I wasn't sure we would win again after freshman year, and especially sophomore year, so that win really was a surprise to me and a message to other schools that Penn is and will be a dynasty for years to come."

The chemistry between the captain and other two players on stage is crucial for a team to win a state championship in Academic Super Bowl. No one-man team wins a state title. Laura Pajot noted this as a salient feature of the '99 state finals: "We had worked together better than ever before, and Missy and I were happy because Mason accepted our input on one answer, even though he disagreed, and we got the point. Also, at one point, Mason just pulled the answer to one question we had no clue on out of the air somehow."

As Penn celebrated its return to championship form, the Kingsmen could also look back on their achievements. With a 51-2 record, the social studies team had claimed its third state title in four years.

For the three seniors on the team, the championship was laden with significance. Mason O'Dell and Jason Ridenour achieved the unprecedented feat in Penn High School history of winning two team state championships within a week, taking the Quiz Bowl title the previous Saturday. O'Dell captained both championship efforts. For Peterson, it was his third state title as a member of the social studies team.

What were the essential ingredients of this championship run? Penn team members in 1999 responded to these questions similarly to what their predecessors in 1996 and 1997 would have. Hard work became the dominant theme in their commentary. "We simply outworked our competition. We worked hard in practice everyday. Our seniors wanted to win bad enough and we did," observed Vander Heyden. According to Pajot, "We practiced exhaustively. I expect that we put at least twice as much work into learning and reviewing the material as the other teams did."

Werts suggested that the attitude motivating all this work was also important: "Our victory came from not only a large amount of work but also from the fact that we never became complacent. Even if we thought we knew something, we'd go over it again. We never took anything for granted."

Mason O'Dell asserted, "We won because we prepared to win. After not winning the year before, it became an obsession to prove that we were the best."

Eight months after the applause had ended at Pike High School and the state championship trophy had been added to Penn's display case, the students reflected on their achievement. Pride understandably was a common theme. Kyle Fisher explained, "I feel proud. I feel that I have something to show that few people have. I can say 'Hey I'm just as good as the football team or the soccer team.' It was worth the time and effort. I carry that feeling with me."

Michelle Werts added, "People recognize the fact that you're a state champion and are generally impressed. This reaction makes all of the hardwork and sacrifice pay off. A state championship gives me a great sense of pride and makes me feel like I'm a success."

Laura Pajot saw it also in terms of validation: "Winning the state championship meant a concrete proof in the benefits of hard work and review."

John Peterson described his thoughts: "I have been on four academic teams that have gone to state, and three have won. It's a sort of familiar thing. Like coming home with something you know belongs to you but you had to go find first."

"It is a great feeling to know that you are the best of the best in the state," remarked Mike Vander Heyden.

Trent McNeer took the most long-term perspective of any on the team when he said, "I look forward to telling my grandkids of my accomplishments and what it is like to be a state champ."

The social studies championship was the last academic title for Penn in the 1998-99 school year. Winning two state crowns in a week was a remarkable enough accomplishment, but Kingsmen academic competitors sought one more state title before 1999 slipped into history.

Hoosier Academic Spell Bowl

Like the Quiz Bowl team, the 1999 Penn Hoosier Academic Spell Bowl team did what none of its predecessors had been able to do: win the state championship.

What seemed an impossible feat two or three seasons before--when Penn was not able to even qualify for the state finals--became realistic after the 1998 Spell Bowl team finished fifth in the state and had 13 of 15 spellers returning for the 1999 campaign. With another year of experience and some new recruits, the 1999 Kingsmen, coached by Pete De Kever, knew they could make a serious run at the state championship, a belief shared by team member Susie Lee: "At the beginning of the season we knew that we could do it. We were confident." The distant dream had finally come within their grasp. The 1999 Penn team would stand at the summit of Indiana Spell Bowl.

Like Academic Super Bowl, Spell Bowl is sponsored by Indiana Academic Competitions for Excellence. Each year, students receive a new list of 3500 words that could be asked in competition. Spell Bowl competitions consist of ten rounds of nine words, each student spelling one round. Spellers have fifteen seconds to write each word after it has been said aloud twice and used in a sentence. Competing in 1999 were 207 high schools in Indiana.

Because some veterans chose not to participate in 1999, the Kingsmen had a smaller team than expected. What they lacked in quantity, though, they would more than make up for in quality. The final team roster included senior Kelsey Schilling, juniors Mike Vorenkamp, Jeff Kish, Dan Wasikowski, and Susie Lee, sophomores Christina Chapman, Charis Heisey, Kent Campbell, Krystal Languell, and Jenni Morrow, and freshmen Stacey Carmichael and Daniel Ernsberger.

Penn's long road to the state finals at Warren Central High School began formally on August 27, with the team's first practice. The Kingsmen practice regimen was much the same as in years past: practice four days per week from 2:45 to 4:00 PM, a 75-word practice test, and time spent writing each word on the list once. Dan Wasikowski cited the value of these daily practice tests: "Actually taking a spelling test is much more like the real competition than reviewing words."

Remaining time was used for occasional board races, spelling words with Alphabits cereal, and writing sentences that included as many list words as possible. Kent Campbell observed, "Alphabits made the difference. Alphabits made me look at words I thought or assumed I knew how to spell and made me realize that I didn't."

Team members also created specialty word lists to help with the trickier types of words, such as words ending in **ance/ence** and **or/er**, capitalized words, and words borrowed from foreign languages. According to Mike Vorenkamp, "The most effective preparation was the specialty list. The lists pulled out words that were similar-- either in sound, spelling, or ending-- and put them in an easy to study list."

Hard work and preparation were hallmarks of the 1999 Spell Bowl team. Charis Heisey recalled, "Writing the thousands upon thousands of words and testing over them was basically the way we pounded it all into our brains...We worked hard. Excessively." Christina Chapman echoed this theme: "Writing the list once through really helped me to become familiar with the list. Practice four days a week was important in keeping on top of the words and not forgetting them." Krystal Languell added, "The fact that we'd been through every word on the list together was why there weren't really any surprises at any of our competitions, including state finals." Stacey Carmichael remarked, "We were just better prepared than the other teams."

A common feature of championship teams is their unity, or chemistry, which the 1999 Penn Spell Bowl team illustrates. Lee explained, "Even if I didn't want to be at practice, being with the team reminded me that we were working to be #1." According to Campbell, "We're like a weird family of brothers and sisters. We are close to each other, but we still have fun and make jokes about each other...Spending that much time with eleven or so other people almost forces you to become close or at least closer friends with them than you were previously." The team also made jokes about the words and gave each other nicknames that sounded like dwarfs' names, using Spell Bowl words like **frumpy**, **sultry**, and **mufti**. This brought much amusement and strengthened the team's identification with each other.

Before the first meet, the team held an intersquad competition, using words from the 1994 regional and state finals, overhead transparencies, and actual competition answer blanks. It was good preparation, but the Kingsmen were itching for some real opponents by the end of September.

Penn's first victims of 1999 came from the Duneland Conference, at their annual meet, held at Merrillville High School. Penn scored a 9 in the first round, trailed briefly after the second round, but then never looked back, cruising to an 84-76 victory over Valparaiso. This was Penn's second consecutive Duneland Meet championship, and the Kingsmen score set a school record for invitationals. Perfect scores came from Kish, Campbell, Lee, Wasikowski, and Morrow. In addition to Valpo, eight other teams were run over by Penn's "high-octane offense": Merrillville, LaPorte, Andrean, Chesterton, Michigan City, Portage, Marquette, and Hobart. It was an auspicious start to the season.

Wasikowski described the importance of the Duneland Meet for Penn: "At the beginning of the year, I think we all knew we were a good team but we didn't start to realize our full potential until our first conference meet. At each meet then we became more confident that we could go the distance."

The Duneland Meet was also memorable for Chapman, a first-year team member: "The first competition was very exciting because it was my first and everyone was doing well. When I was the only one to spell **vignette** right, I was so proud of myself."

A week later, Penn faced a tougher test at the North Central Conference Meet, where host Logansport and perennial power Martinsville provided the main competition. Penn struggled early but never missed another word from the fifth speller on, correctly spelling

Members of the Penn Spell Bowl team participate in their final practice before the 1999 regional, under the banners of past academic state championships. Left to right: Dan Wasikowski, Kelsey Schilling, Jeff Kish, Mike Vorenkamp, Kent Campbell

54 consecutive words. The Berries were crushed under the relentless Penn pressure, and for the first time in years--if ever-- Penn outscored Martinsville in head-to-head competition, 85-78. This victory impressed Jenni Morrow: "When we beat Martinsville, I can remember thinking, 'Wow!' That was when I really knew we had a good chance of winning state."

At the North Central meet, Penn tied the school record for points in a Spell Bowl competition and set a new school invitational record. Languell commented, "What kept surprising me was that in each invitational we were breaking records from the previous year." Perfect scorers at the North Central meet were Kish, Heisey, Lee, Vorenkamp,

The Penn spellers won the regional and were ready to make a run for their first state title.
back: Coach Pete De Kever, Dan Wasikowski, Jeff Kish, Mike Vorenkamp, Susie Lee
middle: Daniel Ernsberger, Charis Heisey, Stacey Carmichael, Krystal Languell
front: Christina Chapman, Jenni Morrow, Kent Campbell, Kelsey Schilling

Languell, Wasikowski, and Morrow. Other schools defeated by the Kingsmen were Kokomo, Delphi, Marion, Lafayette Jeff, Caston, and Peru.

A week later at the regional, the 17-0 Kingsmen met their strongest challenge: John Glenn High School, perennially the best Spell Bowl team in northern Indiana. The Falcons had been outscored by Penn at the 1998 regional, but had beaten Penn at the state finals. The two evenly matched teams treated Spell Bowl fans to a classic duel in the John Glenn gymnasium on October 18. Glenn and Penn were tied through the early rounds, until Glenn stumbled on **Erie** in the fourth round when Campbell was spelling for the Kingsmen. "The best moment was being the only person to stand up for a perfect score at regionals in my round. It was kind of an ego trip," he recalled.

Penn refused to relinquish its one-word lead the rest of the competition, handling the pressure well to come out on top 87-86. Perfect scores were posted by Kish, Campbell, Heisey, Vorenkamp, Languell, Wasikowski, and Morrow. Improving to 27-0, Penn also outscored New Prairie, Mishawaka, Rochester, Bremen, Riley, Caston, Washington, Plymouth, and LaSalle.

Jeff Kish remembered the regional victory: "Every victory was exciting and self-satisfying, but winning regional probably was the best moment before state."

Penn learned the next day it had qualified for the state finals with the second highest score in the state, behind Martinsville's impressive 90. Kingsmen spellers entered the state finals as contenders, but not as favorites. They expected it would take perfection on November 13 to defeat the Artesians and to dethrone defending champion East Noble. John Glenn also was expected to again present a formidable challenge, motivated to avenge the regional loss.

In 1998 Penn also came out of the regional with the second highest score in the state, just behind East Noble on a tiebreaker. However, three other teams (Glenn, Martinsville, and Garrett), two of which Penn had beaten earlier, pulled ahead of Penn in the state finals. Simply put, the 1998 Kingsmen had been outworked and did not handle the pressure as well as the perennial state finalists did.

In 1999 Penn learned from its 1998 performance, vowing that none of the other 29 state finalists would outwork the Kingsmen. "We wanted it more than the other teams," asserted Kent Campbell. In addition to student-led 100-word practice tests, team members would write 50 words of their choosing and take a 75-word lightning round to end each practice. Practices were also lengthened to 4:15 PM. These were intense, exhausting sessions, with team members spelling 225 words per practice. If a student needed to do a make-up for a missed practice, they might be at school until 5:00 PM and could spell up to 400 words in an afternoon. Through more than 45 practices, Penn spellers wrote over 7500 words, as well as writing each word on the list once. To borrow Charis Heisey's word, it was "harshness."

Christina Chapman described the importance of this intense pre-finals preparation: "That last week and even the last day and hour were very significant in the studying process. Not only did it help me to review, it boosted my self-confidence because I knew that even if we did do terrible at state finals, I had done my best and learned to spell many new words."

When November 13 dawned, the Kingsmen were as ready as they were going to be to take on the state's best. This was especially so after a "rise-and-shine" busride practice list of 175 words as the sun cast its first light over US 31 and the central Indiana landscape. Penn began the day as contenders but would end it as state champions.

In Round 1, Kish led off Penn with a perfect score, followed by Kelsey Schilling missing **hobgoblin** at the start of Round 2. This miss took some of the wind out of the Kingsmen's sails, since they presumed a perfect score would be required to win the championship.

Now Penn was playing to not miss any more, hoping that an 89 would be enough for an outside shot at a championship or at least a runner-up. **Hobgoblin** was the first and last word the Kingsmen would miss, as they correctly spelled the next eighty consecutive words. For Jeff Kish, "The largest highlight was when we missed that single word. We all thought it was over, but we hung in there and played it out." Schilling kept focused and spelled the rest of his words correctly. Penn trailed by one, though.

Disappointed at being behind, the Kingsmen tried to stay optimistic. "After Kelsey missed **hobgoblin**, I really thought we wouldn't have a chance, but I remember trying to keep a positive attitude and trying to cheer on everybody as they went up for their turns," Heisey recalled.

Chapman was the third speller and had her career-high score in a crucial round that kept Penn in the hunt. Campbell scored a nine in round four, and Heisey followed with another perfect score, which helped Penn close the gap with Bloomington South. Susie Lee followed with a nine, as one by one the rest of the field began to drop back, unable to match Penn's perfect spelling.

The competition was shaping up as a battle between Penn and Bloomington South, both schools now tied for several rounds. During Mike Vorenkamp's Round 7, the Panthers missed again, and Penn claimed sole possession of first, 62-61. Carmichael saw this as a "defining moment," and Lee agreed: "[When] Bloomington South missed, we could hardly contain our excitement. I knew then that we were going to win."

Vorenkamp described the emotional state finals: "State finals can be likened to a rollercoaster. As we won one competition after another our confidence slowly rose higher and higher. By the time we reached state finals we were at the top. But as Kelsey missed **hobgoblin** we plummeted down, down, down. Would the ride stop here? As I stepped up to the stage I could feel a change. This rollercoaster was going back up. As I spelled word after word I could feel it. This coaster was rising faster and faster. And as I stood up to leave I knew it wasn't going back down."

Languell helped Penn open up a two-point lead, with Northeast Dubois and North Knox the closest pursuers.

Wasikowski also scored a nine, giving Penn an 80-78 lead after nine rounds.

Jenni Morrow came up in Round 10 with all the pressure and excitement of spelling for a state title. While the rest of the field hoped Penn would miss two words, the Kingsmen knew that would not happen. Penn clinched when Morrow spelled the eighth word correct, and the

This photo of the 1999 Penn Spell Bowl team today hangs on the Wall of Champions in the Penn High School Hall of Fame.

Kingsmen celebrated when she raised her hand after the last word, **verisimilitude**. Morrow explained her feelings at this moment: "Once I got the last word and it was one that I knew I knew, I was smiling and I couldn't stop. Actually, mostly I was just relieved that I hadn't let the team down. But I knew I was prepared, so I hadn't been worried. I had pretty much known we would win; that was the best part."

Final score: Penn 89, North Knox and Northeast Dubois 87.

The dream had come true.

Penn had rewritten its record books on the way to the state title. The 89 set a new school Spell Bowl record, as did the incredible nine perfect scores. The Spell Bowl team ended its season 56-0 and staked its claim to being one of Penn's greatest state championship teams.

It was a triumph not only of hard work but also of team work. Mike Vorenkamp described this: "Our victory was due to individual strength. However, a building can not be supported by only one beam. It needs them all in order to stand." Jeff Kish added, "One of the greatest advantages in any sport or competition is teamwork. Had one not done their part, we would not have won. We all did it together."

What does it mean to be a state champion? Everyone has different answers to this question, and three months after their victory in Indianapolis, Penn Spell Bowl team members shared their perspective.

Dan Wasikowski gave his outlook: "To be a part of this team was a great honor and still is. More than that, it has taught me that success really has no bounds. If you believe in yourself, you can achieve anything."

"Penn wins so many state championships that it becomes an everyday occurrence. However, I have a different feeling now that I am a member of a state championship team. Being rewarded for our hard work is wonderful. It motivates me to win again," stated Susie Lee.

Spell Bowl changed first-year team member Charis Heisey's feelings about Penn High School: "Being on the state champ Spell Bowl team really improved my school spirit. I felt like I was recognized as part of Penn, an individual in the 3000."

Penn's only senior, Kelsey Schilling, put the championship in the larger context of his Spell Bowl career: "I think it's really great that I've had the opportunity to win a state championship. I've been on other teams that just didn't cut it, and now I know what it's like…It's just another experience that will add to my well-rounded self."

Thoughts about the championship inevitably led team members to reexamine the effort they invested to get to that point, as Christina Chapman suggested: " I feel very proud of our accomplishments and also our school. A lot of people don't realize that a lot of work goes into preparing to spell. Dedication means you give your all, and our team really gave it all to get to state, and to win it took all we had and then some."

Like their counterparts on the Quiz Bowl and social studies teams, students on the 1999 Spell Bowl team were highly motivated to earn a state championship ring, given by the Penn Booster Club. Mike Vorenkamp observed that these rings became a permanent reminder to the students of their achievement: "It gives me a great deal of pride and satisfaction to wear the ring of a state champion."

In 1999 Penn spellers demonstrated the winning combination of experience, confidence, teamwork, and intense preparation, the ingredients that made Indiana's best Spell Bowl team.

The Spell Bowl championship capped off an amazing year that included five state championships for Penn: Quiz Bowl, Academic Super Bowl social studies, softball, soccer, and Spell Bowl. In the final weeks of the decade, the Kingsmen spellers had brought home one more state championship trophy to Mishawaka. It was a fitting way to end one of the most dominant years any Indiana high school had ever compiled in extracurricular competition.

1999 belonged to the Kingsmen.

Penn High School
Quiz Bowl

Season Record (18-0)
1998-99

Penn	320	Adams	185
Penn	285	Clay	210
Penn	365	Elk. Central	120
Penn	485	LaSalle	270
Penn	270	Marian	175
Penn	325	Mishawaka	185
Penn	305	New Prairie	150
Penn	210	Riley	180
Penn	385	St. Joseph's	190
Penn	325	Washington	195

St. Joseph Valley League Tourney

Penn	290	Washington	115
Penn	230	St. Joseph	215
Penn	340	Adams	210

State Finals (Brownsburg)

Penn	295	Shelbyville	135
Penn	285	Perry Meridian	180
Penn	265	Cardinal Ritter	185
Penn	355	Center Grove	185
Penn	195	Andrean	180

Penn High School
Hoosier Academic Super Bowl
Social Studies

Season Record (51-2)
1998-1999

Warsaw Invitational

Penn	21	Wawasee	18
		Bethany Christian	18
		Warsaw	16
		Bremen	15

Goshen	15
Mishawaka	15
Plymouth	14
NorthWood	13
Jimtown	12
Northridge	9
Concord	9

Duneland Academic Conference Meet (Valparaiso)

Penn	14	Michigan City	16
		Andrean	14
		Valparaiso	11
		Marquette	10
		Mishawaka	9
		LaPorte	8
		Crown Point	8
		Chesterton	8
		Merrillville	8
		Portage	8
		Hobart	7

Regional (LaPorte)

Penn	19	Michigan City	17
		Mishawaka	16
		Valparaiso	16
		Chesterton	14
		LaPorte	13
		Portage	12
		Elkhart Central	11
		Elkhart Memorial	9

State Finals (Indianapolis)

Penn	23	Greencastle	22
		West Lafayette	20
		Elkhart Baptist	20
		Delphi	19
		Avon	18
		Reitz	18
		North Central	18
		Bishop Dwenger	18
		Edgewood	18

Perry Central	18
NorthWood	17
Rushville	17
Cowan	17
Columbus North	16
Terre Haute South	16
Lafayette Harrison	16
Eastern	16
Indian Creek	16
Southern Wells	16
Rockville	15
Hagerstown	14
Springs Valley	13
Greensburg	12

Penn High School
Hoosier Academic Spell Bowl

Season Record (56-0)
1999

Duneland Academic Conference Meet (Merrillville)

Penn	84	Valparaiso	76
		Merrillville	74
		LaPorte	72
		Andrean	71
		Chesterton	65
		Michigan City	59
		Portage	59
		Marquette	58
		Hobart	35

North Central Conference Meet (Logansport)

Penn	85	Martinsville	78
		Logansport	68
		Kokomo	60
		Delphi	50
		Marion	49
		Lafayette Jeff	49
		Caston	47
		Peru	47

Regional (John Glenn HS)

Penn	87	John Glenn	86
		New Prairie	74
		Mishawaka	74
		Rochester	71
		Bremen	71
		Riley	59
		Caston	59
		Washington	57
		Plymouth	57
		LaSalle	51

State Finals (Indianapolis)

Penn	89	North Knox	87
		Northeast Dubois	87
		Madison Consol.	86
		East Noble	86
		Martinsville	86
		John Glenn	85
		North Posey	85
		Bloomington S.	84
		South Vermillion	84
		North Central	83
		Princeton Comm.	83
		Garrett	83
		Gary West	81
		Valparaiso	80
		Andrean	80
		Merrillville	80
		Kouts	78
		Griffith	77
		Hanover Central	76
		Sullivan	75
		Roncalli	75
		Marquette	74
		Rensselaer	73
		Bishop Dwenger	71
		Evans. Harrison	69
		Attica	69
		Wabash	68
		Clinton Prairie	66
		North Judson	64

CHAPTER 20

"THEY FINISHED LIKE CONQUERORS": PENN HIGH SCHOOL'S 2001 SOCIAL STUDIES STATE CHAMPIONSHIP

In his classic work **Caesar and Christ**, historian Will Durant makes a memorable assertion about the Romans: "They finished like conquerors." This statement also applies to the 2001 Penn High School Academic Super Bowl social studies team.

In ASB, high school students compete in five subject areas-- English, fine arts, math, science, and social studies-- and a sixth inter-disciplinary round. Each year, teams receive an outline that identifies sources and subject-specific topics within a larger annual theme. Students then review those topics and sources for months prior to competitions in the spring, culminating in the state finals in early May.

Competitions consist of 25 multiple-choice questions. Teams of three students have 20 seconds to confer and for the captain to deter-mine the correct response.

By the mid-1990s, Penn High School had become the state power in the social studies competition of ASB. The Kingsmen, coached by Pete De Kever, first qualified for the state finals in 1993, finishing tenth, and returned with undefeated state championship teams in 1996 and 1997. After placing eleventh in the 1998 state contest, Penn won the state title in 1999, and in 2000 defeated Bethany Christian, 23-21, to claim a fourth state crown.

As the 2000-2001 season began, Penn sought to defend its state title, but faced the challenge of returning just two players from the 2000 championship team: Michelle Werts and Jacob Meyer.

Werts, a fourth-year team member, had played on the 1999 state title team and had captained the 2000 championship. Dedicated, bright, and mature, she entered her senior season as perhaps the best Academic Super Bowl player in the state. With a state championship in 2001, Michelle Werts would become the only student in the fifteen-year history of ASB to play on three consecutive social studies state championship teams. As the Penn social studies team was studying Roman history, Werts would be attempting to make Indiana history.

Academic Super Bowl is a collective effort, though, and not even the best player in the state could do it alone. Joining her would be Jacob Meyer, a second-year player who had seen some playing time in 2000 and who had enthusiastically learned from his mentors, Class of 2000 team members Trent McNeer and Mike Vander Heyden. Werts recruited senior Jamie Bitzenhofer, a transfer student from Wyoming, after seeing her potential in the honors government class they had together. Junior Amber Kotyuk and freshmen Joe Brooks, Ilya Gekhtman, Angelica Momotiuk, and Sam Momotiuk rounded out the Penn roster.

As in years past, the social studies team began practices in early September, working through several sources and a study outline of Roman leaders covering the period 148 BC to 180 AD. The Kingsmen regimen included one 75-minute practice per week in the first semester, which, in the second semester, was supplemented with a second after-school practice and 3-hour Sunday practices.

Through the fall and winter, the team steadily gained familiarity with each other and their subject. While all team members were highly enthusiastic and dedicated, Bitzenhofer, Meyer, and Brooks emerged as the core of players likely to join Werts in the competitions. Bitzenhofer brought critical reading skills, Meyer used intensive review sessions at home to steadily grow in his understanding, and Brooks had the most background knowledge on Ancient Rome.

As the season advanced, Michelle Werts grew beyond her captain role of the previous season and became the assistant coach of the team. Three years' experience as captain at Schmucker Middle School and competing at Penn since her freshman year made her eminently qualified for this role. Werts taught her teammates strategies for critically reading and highlighting their sources, explained the theory behind how to participate during a round, and led at least half of the team's review sessions. She also collaborated on determining long-term review strategy and line-ups, and, later in the season, planned and conducted two full practices before the regional and state finals. Werts' expanded role would prove to be a decisive component of the Kingsmen's success in 2001.

By the end of February, the team had been reading, reviewing, and practicing for six months, yet had not faced an opponent.

It was time to compete.

Invitationals and Regional

The Kingsmen faced their first opponents on March 8 at the Warsaw Invitational. The competition began well, as Penn answered the first four questions correctly, before missing question 5, dealing with Nero declaring himself a god. At the break after question 10, Penn had 9, yet trailed already by one point. They correctly answered the next five before missing question 16. Still behind Northwood by one, the Kingsmen put together another run of five correct responses before missing question 23. Penn got the last two questions correct, but it was not enough. Northwood finished with 23, and Dwenger had 22, edging the Kingsmen on a tie-breaker.

Not since 1995 had the social studies team failed to win the first competition of the season. Losing the Warsaw Invitational was a harsh dose of reality for the two-time defending state champions, a reminder that they would not simply be handed the 2001 state championship. They would have to work still harder and smarter, filling in the remaining gaps in their knowledge of Ancient Rome.

Redemption came for the Kingsmen five days later at the Western Invitational in Russiaville. After answering the first five correctly, Penn missed question 6, and answered 7 through 10 right, to stay tied with Elwood. The Kingsmen missed 11 and 13, but led Western 12-11 after question 15. Penn was perfect the rest of the way, winning 22-18 over Western.

After two invitationals, the team had correctly answered 44 of 50 questions in competition and owned a 23-2 record against their opponents. With another month to prepare for the regional, Penn would stand a good chance of qualifying for their sixth consecutive state finals. The loss at Warsaw had been a blessing because it kept the team from getting too confident. The Kingsmen knew they were beatable and that only supreme effort would hold off their opponents.

The April 17 regional at LaPorte High School started off on the wrong note for Penn and every other team. The first question asked students to identify the "most constant, public, and practical sign of the Roman will to power." None of the nine teams answered correctly. The Kingsmen bounced back to get question 2, but then missed question 3, dealing with Tiberius Gracchus' "untraditional act." The answer given by the question reader was dissolving the Senate, but the Penn players knew that was incorrect and chose his standing for immediate re-election.

Missing two of the first three was not the ideal way to start the competition, but after getting questions 4 and 5 correct, Penn stood in a three-way tie for first. After the rough start, they were perfect from questions 4 through 10 and held a one-point lead over Valparaiso and Elkhart Central at the time-out. The Kingsmen hoped the worst part of the round was past.

But that would not be so.

After the substitution, Penn missed questions 11 through 13, the only time a Penn social studies team had ever missed three consecutive questions in a competition. Kingsmen fans were starting to worry, not only about whether they could hold a lead to win the regional, but whether their score would qualify for state.

Penn answered 14 and 15 correctly to stand tied with Valparaiso at 10. Seemingly unable to put together another streak of right answers, the Kingsmen were correct on 16, missed 17, and then rebounded to get 18 through 20 correct. They held a 14-13 lead over Valpo after question 20.

Penn missed question 21, though, when they did not know that Gaius Gracchus offered citizenship to all Latins. But that would be the last incorrect question of the evening, as the Kingsmen rallied to answer the final four questions correctly.

Penn had retained its regional crown with an 18-14 victory over Valparaiso. The Vikings, tied with the Kingsmen after question 15,

On April 17, 2001, the Penn ASB social studies team won their sixth consecutive regional championship.
standing: Captain Michelle Werts, Jamie Bitzenhofer, Jacob Meyer, Joe Brooks, Amber Kotyuk
kneeling: Sam Momotiuk, Angelica Momotiuk, Ilya Gekhtman

collapsed in the final ten, missing four of the last five questions. Penn's record stood at 31-2.

The 2001 regional was a grueling ordeal, and the Penn players felt fortunate to come away with an 18 and their sixth consecutive regional championship. The next day they learned that their score was the highest of all 300 schools around the state, with the nearest competitors at only 16. For the first time in its history, the Penn social studies team would head into the state finals ranked #1 in the state.

State Finals

On May 5, 2001, the Academic Super Bowl state finals were again held in Indianapolis at the Pike Performing Arts Center. Twenty-six schools in four enrollment classes would compete for the state championship.

Leaving Penn High School at 6 AM, the social studies team began a three-hour practice and review session.

They would need every minute.

Michelle Werts leads teammates Sam Momotiuk, Joe Brooks, and Jacob Meyer during practice the day before the 2001 social studies state finals.

The Penn social studies team completes a final review before competing in the state finals at the Pike Performing Arts Center in Indianapolis.

A year of hopes, preparation, and teamwork would all come down to 25 multiple-choice questions.

When Jacob Meyer later recalled his experience at the state finals, he described the team's feelings before the round began: "Obviously, when we first sat down, we all were just kind of really nervous. We were shaking out the jitters, like, 'We're cool, we're cool. We're gonna do this.' From that very first question, before it went up, me and Michelle and Jamie kind of looked at each other and said, 'We're gonna win this, no matter what it takes.' We knew we were going to win, and we knew we could make it."

Rather than a dream come true, the state finals round began more like a nightmare.

Penn missed the first question, not knowing that veterans were the most forceful group demanding vengeance after Julius Caesar's assassination. The Kingsmen answered correctly the second question, about Romans being grateful to Augustus, but then missed the third, dealing with Augustus' rule. Penn trailed by two points to several teams.

"The first couple questions kind of scared us because, you know, we didn't make 'em," Meyer remembered.

Penn bounced back to get number four correct, but then stumbled again on five, when they did not know Spartacus was Thracian. After five questions the Kingsmen were in the back half of the field, well behind the leader, Frontier, 5-2.

Missing three of the first five questions was certainly not how Penn had scripted the beginning of the state finals. In some years past, they had gotten nine or even ten of the first ten questions. In 1999 and 2000, Penn's scores were 23 of 25 correct, so their missed questions had been rare. This was shaping up to be a disaster. The questions were difficult, and the Kingsmen were just not getting them right. After those first five questions, the Penn faithful knew they were in trouble, being down by three. That was by no means, though, an insurmountable deficit so early in the competition, especially since they could tie a team late in the round and win on the tiebreaker, which favored performance in the last five questions.

Five days after state, Michelle Werts and Jamie Bitzenhofer watched a video of the state finals and shared their recollections of how the team answered the final fifteen questions.

Despite trailing early, Werts recalled, "During the first ten, I wasn't really concerned yet." Nonetheless, "Since we fell behind early on, we knew that every question was critical if we were to prevail in the end."

From question 6 through question 11, Penn was flawless and seemed to have gotten into a rhythm.

Missing question 12 was the low point of the competition for the Kingsmen. Students needed to identify that Cicero was named because of a wart on his nose.

For the Cicero question, Bitzenhofer said, "I knew this."

"You didn't display any confidence there, Jamie," Werts noted.

"No, because I wasn't sure of it, but it seemed right."

"And we all looked at Jamie, it was like--"

"Well, I remember it was from ninth grade, and I remember something about warts," Bitzenhofer explained.

"It was like, 'Jamie, what's **Cicero** mean in Latin.' She goes, 'I don't know.'"

"I remembered warts but I wasn't sure of it."

Going into question 13, Penn trailed Elmhurst by three points. That deficit so late in the state finals was like being behind by three touchdowns in the third quarter of a state championship football game. Worried though the team was, all they could do was look forward to the next question, hoping that it would be difficult and true to what they had studied and that Elmhurst and other teams ahead of them would miss it. Only that way could Penn climb back into contention.

According to Michelle Werts, "About question 13, though, when we were down by three, I just remember saying, 'Unless these get harder, there's no way you can come back from a three-point deficit at this caliber of competition.'"

With some dramatic overstatement, Jamie Bitzenhofer remembered, "I was sitting there thinking, 'I'm such a loser. I'm up there and I'm not doing well, and it's my fault.'"

Jacob Meyer explained his feelings at this crucial moment: "When we were down by three really, really scared us. This idea that we aren't invincible kind of scared me. We went into this extremely cocky, knowing we were going to win. In those moments, I swear God was playing a prank on us. He was like, 'Oh really, you think you're going to win?' It's like it's inevitable we're going to win, but the road was a little harder. And I think it made it all the better."

After this low point, Werts and her teammates did what was needed: get the questions right. After the miss on question 12, they got 11 straight questions correct. The Penn captain recalled, "I didn't know it was eleven in a row. We just knew we were catching up."

"But the questions got harder, and as we went, we just kept getting and getting more and more, and we kept closing the gap and closing the gap, just like a scripted play," Meyer described.

Werts and Bitzenhofer remembered their deliberations for question 18, which required students to know that Romans were not masters of papermaking.

Bitzenhofer recalled, "I knew this...'papermaking' and she's like, 'Posters? They didn't make posters.'"

"I was thinking in contemporary terms...like posters. I'm like, 'Jamie, if you don't have paper, how do you have posters?'" responded Werts.

"So I'm saying paper because they used papyrus and they used scrolls and stuff, and she's like, 'Posters?'"

"I just had a problem with the word **posters**, okay?!" Werts laughed.

"And finally I turn around and I go, 'It's propaganda,'" said Bitzenhofer.

"And then I was like, 'Okay,'" and the captain put down papermaking as the team's answer.

Penn also correctly answered question 19, asking them to identify which was not a nickname of Sulla. According to Bitzenhofer, "That's just basic knowledge of Sulla."

On the next question, students had to identify that one of the powers of the **pater familias** was not granting citizenship to his wife.

Bitzenhofer remembered, "'Cause his wife wasn't getting citizenship no matter what."

"It's like, 'A is correct, B is correct, C is correct. Oh, it's D,'" Werts explained.

"Citizenship wasn't given to women, " added Bitzenhofer.

"But it was a government thing," Werts replied. "I remembered A directly and C."

Penn's string of correct answers enabled them to pull within one point of Elmhurst, 17-16, after question 20. As question 21 began, the Kingsmen started keeping track of their right and wrong answers versus Elmhurst's in the final five, in case it came down to a tie-breaker. But that could only happen if Penn continued to get their questions right and Elmhurst missed one. The Kingsmen wished for a way to play defense, but could only hope for difficult questions that played to their strengths, topics that they had thoroughly studied.

Question 21 dealt with Augustus banishing Ovid, rather than three other writers. This posed no problem, according to Jamie Bitzenhofer: "They said Horace, Livy, Virgil, Ovid. Who do you think? He liked the other three."

The next question tested students' knowledge of term lengths for Roman senators by comparing them to those of American government officials. Werts described how the team worked through this question: "Jacob...would point to one of these like-- this happened before she even said, 'Begin.' He pointed to one. He said, 'The President.' Then he stopped and looked, 'No, no, no.' Then he pointed to B, Supreme Court justices. And when she said, 'Begin,' he's like, 'Life terms.' And I'm like, 'Well, that's B.' And Jamie says, 'I agree.'"

Bitzenhofer's years of watching **Sesame Street** played a role in getting question 23 right. It asked for which of the statements about Roman slavery was not correct. She explained, "This is the 'one of these things is not like the others.' That's how we got it."

"It was also like the others were all so specific. A was so general," Werts added.

Bitzenhofer continued, "How I got it was, one was about slavery was increasing and one was about the implosion of slavery, so it's got to be one of those two because they're exact opposites. I literally said when that question came up, 'One of these things is not like the others.'"

After question 23, Penn and Elmhurst were tied, with Angola and Bethany Christian just a point back. If the Kingsmen missed no more, they would win on the first tie-breaker.

It would not be so easy, though.

Question 24 asked for which group would have opposed Julius Caesar. The girls' first instincts were correct, but Meyer convinced them into going with an incorrect response.

The captain explained what happened, laughing, "Oops. Jacob talked us out of it. Jamie and I both said C, aristocracy. We're like, 'Oh, it's aristocracy, hands-down, no-doubt. Everybody else liked the **pax Romana**.' But then Jacob said something about **pax** would be peace and the merchants got their trade from wars, and so I'm like, 'Oh, that makes sense,' and so we put D. And then we looked and nobody moved, and we're like, 'Okay. It's okay. We're still tied.'"

Bitzenhofer described her thinking: "I was sitting there in my mind. I'm going, 'Could we get the tie-breaker? Could we?'"

"Yeah, that's what I was thinking. I was saying to myself, I knew that we had the Class 2 school on the tie-breaker because I knew that we had caught up in those last-- but I didn't know about Bethany Christian. I didn't know about them on the tie-breakers," Werts added.

According to Jacob Meyer, after question 24, "We were extremely down, and I think it was almost dead silence. It was my fault. My fault-- I missed it. They went against what they had originally said to my answer, and we missed it. Right there, I wanted to die. But it was okay. There was this feeling of, 'Who cares if we win or lose. We had so much fun, we don't care.' At that point we cared, but we had too much fun to be brought down."

In the few seconds between questions, the team had no time to articulate these thoughts. Meyer recalled them only saying "short little phrases like, 'We can do it, we'll do it.' There was no major discussion, and even if there was time, we wouldn't have been. We were so scared. It was just amazing."

One simple gesture by the Penn captain spoke volumes, though. Meyer described how Werts "cupped her hands around her nose and partially around her eyes. Seeing that, oh, I just wanted to melt away right then. It was so terrible. It was just such a terrible feeling, and I knew we had to have 25, or we wouldn't have won."

Penn's miss had stuck them in a three-way tie at 19, with Bethany and Elmhurst, but Bethany Christian and other teams with 18 had taken Penn's tie-breaker advantage away. If the score ended up tied after the last question, the Kingsmen would lose the state championship on the first tie-breaker, which is the number of correct answers in questions 21-25.

A year of dreaming and hundreds of accumulated hours' investment by the Penn team boiled down to the last question. It had been much easier for the Kingsmen in 2000, when, having clinched on question 24, they were able to coast through question 25, which they could miss without risk. While that would have been the less stressful way to end the quest for three-in-a-row, it lacked the intensity of this situation. Here, on the last question of the state finals, the last question and final minute of Michelle Werts' illustrious ASB career, the fate of Penn's season would be decided. While the interval between questions 24 and 25 was so short that Penn players and fans did not have opportunity to think all these thoughts at that time, in retrospect the high drama of the moment becomes manifest.

While it was a team effort all the way to the end, the final burden of responsibility for choosing the right answer rested on Werts' shoulders. Nobody in the state was better to have in that position than Michelle Werts. She had been preparing for that moment for not just a year, but for four years, even seven years, since her ASB career had begun at Schmucker Middle School.

The captain commented on her feelings during the round: "The state finals were extremely nerve-wracking. I'm sure that all of the emotions felt in the audience were mirrored on stage."

When question 25 flashed on the screen, the Kingsmen knew it was reasonably challenging:

> *The most astonishing thing about Trajan compared to Tiberius, Nero, and Domitian was that he believed all of the following EXCEPT*
> *A. It is better that the guilty go unpunished than the innocent be condemned.*
> *B. The Lord of the state should be the first servant of that state.*
> *C. Liberty is better than order.*
> *D. A man can never really own anything.*

The answer was C, an incorrect form of a quote the team had often studied, including that morning as they covered their review guides one last time.

Werts described what happened during the 15-second conferring period: "Jacob pointed to it immediately, and that's what I was thinking, and that's what Jamie was thinking. And we had a couple good reasons. He was straight-out conservative and that's so liberal."

Bitzenhofer added, "And I'm sitting here thinking, 'That's a quote--

top of the page.'" She was right. The question writer had drawn the question from the first line of page 410 of **Caesar and Christ**, which said Trajan "preferred order to liberty and power to peace." Throughout the season Bitzenhofer had joked about how her teammates could remember where certain ideas were located on a page. She would tell them that was too concrete-sequential for her, but by the end of the season, she, too, knew the sources so well that she thought about them like the rest of the team did.

Werts continued to explain her reasoning: "It didn't apply to Trajan at all. He was conservative, and that was liberty is better than order. Any conservative is not going to say that liberty is better than order. That's all. Even at the time of the American Revolution, that was really liberal. Order, military, order-- it just didn't even apply."

"On the last question, I knew it. I knew the answer was C-- was just amazing. I really felt like I contributed to the team. My pencil was there first, and I was very proud of that," Jacob Meyer remembered. "I knew Trajan was the best." Having blamed himself for missing question 24, Meyer felt redeemed by the final question.

Of the three teams tied at 19, only Penn answered the last question correct. Dwenger, Angola, Elmhurst, and Bethany all finished with 19. Had the Kingsmen missed the last question, they would have finished fourth because of tie-breakers. Had Dwenger, Bethany Christian, or Angola gotten it right, they would have won the title.

When the scoreboard showed Penn in first, Jamie Bitzenhofer was the first to scream in exultation.

Jacob Meyer described the moment: "We pulled it off and we won, and that last question was positively the best moment of my entire life. When Jamie screams and me and Michelle just grabbed each other's hands and just go crazy because we knew we won. And then after that moment, we were all just like, 'Wait a second, did we actually win?' and we had to go back up and verify, but we did and it was amazing that we pulled that off. There was nothing more exhilarating than that. It was like we all went into a seizure mode, just shaking, going crazy...The last question about Trajan was the awesomest question. When we got it right, we went nuts because at that point we were able to say that we worked hard **and** achieved our goal, which was 'Win it for Missy!'"

Michelle Werts told the **Elkhart Truth**, "When [the score] popped up that we won, everybody gave each other a group hug."

Bitzenhofer remembered, "And then I calmed down. That's when I wrote **booyah** down. That was the 'booyah moment.'" During the competitions that spring, the team had come up with this term to represent the moment when they knew they had clinched a victory.

"You did it right after I finished figuring [the score] out. You're sitting there, you're like, 'Oh, booyah!' You had to put the obligatory **booyah**," Werts reminded Bitzenhofer.

"This was like, 'I'm smart. I'm now officially smart,'" Bitzenhofer joked.

Penn High School, 2001 Academic Super Bowl social studies state champions
back: Sam Momotiuk, Angelica Momotiuk
front: Jamie Bitzenhofer, Joe Brooks, Michelle Werts, Jacob Meyer, Amber Kotyuk, Ilya Gekhtman, Coach Pete De Kever

Werts added, "This was the most exciting competition of all of them."

After the round, as the other teams were called to receive their awards, only Penn was left on stage. Werts remembered, "Basically the time after the round was spent basking in the glory of our victory. We simply enjoyed the moment while it lasted."

Bitzenhofer added a distinctive metaphor to describe the minutes on stage after the exciting round: "It was like a backrub. That's what it was like. It was really relaxing."

May 5, 2001 became a day that no Penn team member would ever forget. Jamie Bitzenhofer, Joe Brooks, Angelica Momotiuk, Sam Momotiuk, Ilya Gekhtman, and Amber Kotyuk all had their first taste of the Penn tradition of winning a state championship, earning the coveted state ring provided by the Penn Booster Club. Jacob Meyer experienced the thrill of a repeat state title, one that he had contributed to even more than in 2000.

Michelle Werts ended her career the way it was meant to: with the unprecedented threepeat. To do so, she and her teammates had to orchestrate arguably the greatest come-from-behind victory in the history of the Academic Super Bowl state finals. Adding to the drama for the Penn captain was her father, Tom Werts, who had flown to Indianapolis from a sales trip in Los Angeles, arriving at 2 AM Saturday, so that he could see his daughter compete. She and her teammates had rewarded his devotion with the greatest moment in her academic competitions career.

Reflections

Why did the Penn social studies team win the 2001 state championship? Team members shared their answers to this question in the weeks following the state finals.

"I believe we worked the hardest," Michelle Werts asserted. "It was the hard work that translated into success. We also worked as a team; we carried the weight together. I think that a large part of our success in ASB is the ground-pounding. We go over the information until it is permanently imbedded in our brains."

Seniors Jamie Bitzenhofer and Michelle Werts were the brain trust behind the final academic state championship won by Penn High School's talented Class of 2001.

This sentiment was echoed by Jacob Meyer: "We worked our butts off! Our superior knowledge gave us the advantage."

Ilya Gekhtman agreed: "I feel the championship was won due to repetition. This was possible because of the team's commitment to the strenuous practice schedule...I think of it as a testament to the mutual effort of people. I am glad I did not quit when it first became evident that I will not play."

Penn players outworked everybody in the state, but they also won because they had an experienced captain who did not let the pressure of competition bother her, even when it was at its greatest, such as after question 24 of the state finals. Having competed for seven years, including five years as a captain, Michelle Werts was the best-prepared and most-experienced ASB player in the state. She used her intelligence, good memory, and ability to read quickly, think through questions, and make connections. If they had studied and reviewed a topic, she and her teammates would usually have learned it well enough to get the right answer. Werts commented on this to the **South Bend Tribune** after the regional: "We've studied the material so much that you might get a little nervous. But when you put in the work, you know the answer is in there somewhere."

The Kingsmen would also not have won without Jamie Bitzenhofer. She was willing to commit to the team, added so much to the team's morale and cohesiveness, and most importantly, was a good reader and thinker, had much background knowledge, and knew some Latin. Bitzenhofer added an element of destiny to the Kingsmen's quest for the three-peat. Maybe it was meant to be that she would leave her home in Wyoming and come all the way to Indiana, that it would result in more than just a high school diploma.

Werts' influence was also felt through Bitizenhofer's decisive contribution to the team because, by the second or third meeting of government class, the captain saw her potential and recruited her to join the team. Bitzenhofer expressed this well: "As far as ASB goes, I think it was one of the best things I ever got talked into doing. Missy is definitely the right kind of peer pressure."

Jacob Meyer also contributed, not just through the questions he helped the team answer correctly. He had learned enough about how ASB worked during his first year that he was able to help Werts guide the rest of the team. He provided an example to the new students that it was okay to not play much, that their time would come, as his had. Meyer was motivated and became a solid player as he had more opportunity to intensively review the content.

Meyer expressed another essential ingredient of the Kingsmen's state title: "The chemistry our team had was a huge factor. As Missy says, 'You can't have a good movie if the leads don't have chemistry.'" This team chemistry was also enhanced by their competitive success, much humor in practices, and simply spending a lot of time together. Likewise, answering hundreds of practice questions throughout the season contributed in a practical way to the chemistry needed among the players in competition. They practiced the group dynamic, and Werts knew how to judge her teammates' contributions.

The state finals illustrated the importance of each team member. Because Penn won by just a single point, everyone's contribution was vital, not just the three players who competed on May 5. Everyone participated in the practice activities that benefited the whole team. Had any one player performed differently, it might have changed the team dynamic and cost the Kingsmen that one vital point and the state championship. Amber Kotyuk agreed: "I think we won the state championship because of the efforts made by each team member to prepare those playing at state. We read, prepared questions, made games and handouts on the emperors. We certainly were thorough, and I think that is what made all the difference."

Military historians say that the strongest motivating factor for men in combat is "primary group cohesion," or solidarity to the unit, rather than fighting for abstract values such as one's country. This was true for the 2001 Penn social studies team, as well. They were motivated to win for each other, not by winning for Penn or getting another plaque for the school trophy case. The best expression of this sentiment came after the regional when several team members simultaneously asserted their desire to "Win it for Missy!"

This state championship came also from past success. Werts having been to the state finals three previous years and Meyer having been there as a sophomore helped to make the whole experience less intimidating. Pike became a home away from home for the Kingsmen. They also believed they were going to win state, that they needed to win because they had won before. The four previous titles made winning in 2001 seem more achievable, even expected. Tradition offered a tide of momentum to ride.

According to the theory of Harvey Hurst, long-time government teacher at Penn, Werts and her teammates may have won on that last question because they had the higher expectation of needing to win the overall championship rather than a meaningless enrollment-class title. If they were going for just the class title, the Penn players could have quit after question 23. Having won Class 1 by five points in both 1999 and 2000, the Kingsmen knew the real competition would come from the rest of the field, and that proved to be so with Bethany Christian,

Jamie Bitzenhofer, Michelle Werts, and Jacob Meyer were cheered by thousands during the Memorial Day parades in Osceola and Mishawaka following the 2001 state championship.

Elmhurst, Dwenger, and Angola. Penn was driven to work harder because they knew it would take a higher level of performance to defeat the whole field and win a true state championship. Maybe this added imperative helped them get that extra question. Lower expectations from the start may have left the Penn students with an 18 or 19 at state.

What does it mean to have won the 2001 social studies state championship?

"The championship is the representation of a year's hard work," Kotyuk explained. "It is the culmination of energy, time, brainpower, and strength. It is the victory of the final battle in a war."

Meyer noted the championship's self-esteem value: "It means so much to me. I have never been athletic, and my brother and sister have won countless baseball and softball competitions. This was my way to show everyone what I can do."

Academic Super Bowl gave Bitzenhofer a sense of belonging in a school where otherwise she did not know very many people. She explained, "I really love ASB's sense of tradition. I came from a school in Wyoming which absolutely did not excel in anything extracurricular, and I think that made it hard to fit in the school there. There was nowhere to go after school, there wasn't a sense of tradition or of people working together, it was very cold and a hard place to get used to for me. Penn was much better even though it was my senior year, and I think a lot of that was due to ASB and drama.

"I'm not an overly structured person, and ASB forced me to learn how to better handle things like organization (I did better toward the end). I had to learn time management and effective studying. It is definitely a different type of thinking and learning which I think is valuable," she added.

Joe Brooks expressed how the state championship caused his view of being on the team to evolve: "At the beginning, it was the ring, and at the end, the nice addition towards college. It is still all those things, but now it's like I have a commitment to the team, that it's an opportunity and a responsibility to win and put forth all the effort for the team."

Ilya Gekhtman added, "After the victory, I became caught up in the amazing story of the comeback and the year in general."

"Winning the state championship still gives me a warm and fuzzy feeling each time I think about it. It makes me feel that I helped contribute to something that made a lot of people happy," reflected Angelica Momotiuk.

Michelle Werts shared her philosophy: "Any state championship represents the culmination of the efforts made. It is proof that you have become the best in the state. Therefore, any state championship experience is to be honored and treasured. You have become one of the elites."

Werts was well-qualified to speak on the subject of state championships. In addition to three ASB state titles, she had also contributed to four state championships in broadcast journalism. Werts' seven state championships were the most of any individual in the history of Penn High School.

Besides winning, other experiences stood out for team members when they reminisced about the season.

The team did more than just work hard. According to Meyer, "We had so much fun! The time in between the studying is what made us a team. Our entire team had chemistry."

Although she set a state-record for consecutive social studies state championships, Michelle Werts was thinking of her younger teammates when the **Tribune** interviewed her following the state finals round: "We had a lot of new players this year, so I think that is even more important." Later, she commented, "The memory that stands out for me personally is the ability to teach the newcomers about the traditions that surround ASB and being able to watch a team and camaraderie develop."

The 2001 social studies state championship team was distinguished not just by their remarkable comeback at the state finals. More important to their story is the dedication, teamwork, and faith shown by the Penn students throughout their season.

They finished like conquerors.

They won like Kingsmen.

Penn High School
Hoosier Academic Super Bowl
Social Studies

Season Record (56-2)
2000-2001

Warsaw Invitational

Penn	22	Northwood	23
		Dwenger	22
		Concord	17
		Bethany Christian	17
		Goshen	16
		Warsaw	14
		Northridge	14
		Fairfield	13
		Jimtown	12
		Mishawaka	12
		North Miami	11
		Plymouth	11
		Wawasee	11
		Columbia City	8
		Bremen	7

Western Invitational (Russiaville)

Penn	22	Western	18
		Wabash	15
		Elwood	15
		Danville	13
		Taylor	13
		Eastern	12
		North Miami	12
		Peru	10
		Hamilton Heights	9
		Clinton Central	9

Regional (LaPorte)

Penn	18	Valparaiso	14
		Elkhart Central	13
		Portage	11
		LaPorte	10

Michigan City	8
Mishawaka	8
Chesterton	8
Washington	7

State Finals (Indianapolis)

Penn	20	Bethany Christian	19
		Angola	19
		Elmhurst	19
		Dwenger	19
		Brebeuf	18
		North Posey	18
		Seeger	18
		Tri	18
		Richmond	17
		North Decatur	17
		Boone Grove	17
		Delphi	17
		Homestead	15
		South Decatur	15
		Brownsburg	14
		Carmel	13
		Northrop	13
		Frontier	13
		Elwood	12
		Rushville	12
		LaVille	11
		Terre Haute North	8
		River Forest	8
		Central Catholic	8
		Clinton Central	6

ACKNOWLEDGEMENTS

This book is the product of many people's contributions. By sharing their memories, directing me to additional sources, or offering commentary about drafts of essays, they have brought these subjects to life and made their retelling more effective.

Many of these essays could not have been written without the resources of the Mishawaka-Penn-Harris Public Library. Newspapers and census records on microfilm and other reference books were used throughout these writings. The library also loaned me photographs to copy and acquired microfilm from the Carnegie Corporation archives. David Eisen's index of vital statistics from the Mishawaka Enterprise was essential for easily finding birth and death records. David Eisen, Connie Johnson, and other staff of the library's Heritage Center deserve special thanks. The community should be proud that so much of its history can be researched from this facility.

This book also owes much of its content to the writers and editors of the **Mishawaka Enterprise**, **South Bend Tribune**, and other local newspapers. Some of these writers have been dead for over a century, so I am pleased that their work will find a twenty-first century audience through these essays.

Merle Blue merits recognition for his years teaching Mishawaka High School students and for sharing so much of his retirement with the community, researching and writing about local history topics. Merle is Mishawaka's leading expert on the early iron industry here and helped with the Alanson Hurd research. He also provided guidance and information for the Billy Sunday and Robert F. Kennedy essays.

Jeanne Denham has done much research on the Hurd family, which she generously shared to help complete the Hurd essay. One of Hurd's descendants, Jane Patterson, also provided the family's genealogy and the wonderful photos of Alanson and Sarah Hurd.

I am indebted to the extended Powell family for their invaluable help in researching Farrow, Elijah, and their descendants. Much of the information about the Powells came from their family historian, John Charles Bryant. Elijah's great-grandchildren, Bill Roberts and Sandra Roberts Haines, also provided ideas and encouragement. In July 1998 Farrow Powell's descendants held a reunion in South Bend and graciously extended their hospitality to me. It was one of my great thrills as a student of local history to meet descendants and relatives of Elijah Powell. Roger Peterson made possible much of the content about Owen County's African American community, and Owen Garner provided insights about Medora Powell, whom he knew personally.

The interview with Helen Doolittle was initiated by her grandson, Drew Johnson. Mrs. Doolittle kindly shared both her time and memories with me one afternoon in the summer of 2000, and as a result, we have more insight into life in Mishawaka when she was growing up.

The essay about my grandfather results largely from the memories my father passed down to me over the years. Our family is grateful to Wayne Linson, whose oral history interview allowed us to see my grandfather from the perspective of a friend and co-worker. Achiel De Kever provided important memories of the family in the 1910s and 1920s, and Ralph Hillman shared background about the 11th Field Artillery in Hawaii.

Charles Kuhn consented to be interviewed twice for the essay about the Aldrich house. Mr. Kuhn passed away in July 2002, and I am pleased that his boyhood reminiscences live on for the community through this essay.

Dwight and Virginia Snyder shared their time and memories of Mabel Snyder and the Mishawaka Reservoir caretaker's residence, doing much to help the house become a home. Violet Swartzlander and her daughters Sally and Dixie visited the caretaker's residence in the summer of 1996 and told me about their brief time living there more than a half-century before. Glory June Greiff used her expertise to speak on behalf of the house during the National Register review process. Her comments highlight the house's significance and uniquity.

The essay about my return visit to North Side School owes its present form to Linda Brookshire, who taught a class I took at IUSB in the summer of 1992. The essay was originally written as an assignment for that class. Linda's comments transformed the essay into so much more than it originally had been and in the process made me a better writer.

The staff of the First United Methodist Church kindly gave me access to their archives' file about Billy Sunday and allowed me to photograph the altar where Sunday spoke.

While the events surrounding Shelby Shake's final season at Mishawaka High School were largely developed with newspaper articles and the 1937 **Miskodeed**, his story would be less compelling were it not for the insights of Van Norris, Robert Schweisberger, Howard Shake, Arthur Vallicelli, and John Wooden. I am also thankful to Jerry Klaer, who first brought this incident to my attention.

My brother, Andrew De Kever, encouraged me to pursue the story of Private Charles Kuhl and helped me find his grave one cold winter day. Brian Dentino shared his copy of **A Genius for War**, the outstanding Patton biography that puts the slapping incidents into the larger context of Patton's career and the war in Europe.

Much like the Shake–Wooden essay, the story of Francis Hill and the state runner-up cross country teams was given an important personal dimension thanks to interviews with Grace Hill, Jim Lang, Ralph Powell, Stan Ross, Paul Williams, and Don Wood. The cross country alumni, led by Stan Ross, have shown great pride in their school and have been supportive of my efforts to share the story of their team's achievements.

The 1999 and 2001 Penn academic state championship essays resulted largely from interviews or questionnaires from Jamie Bitzenhofer, Joe Brooks, Kent Campbell, Stacey Carmichael, Christina Chapman, Kyle Fisher, Ilya Gekhtman, Charis Heisey, Jeff Kish, Amber Kotyuk, Krystal Languell, Susie Lee, Trent McNeer, Nathan Meng, Jacob Meyer, Angelica Momotiuk, Jenni Morrow, Mason

O'Dell, Laura Pajot, John Peterson, Aaron Rosenfeld, Kelsey Schilling, Mike Vander Heyden, Coach Susan Van Fleit, Mike Vorenkamp, Dan Wasikowski, and Michelle Werts. It was an honor to coach these students and then to write about their achievements.

Mary Renshaw, the former archivist at the Northern Indiana Center for History, was supportive of my efforts to have many of these essays published in the "Through the Years" column of the **South Bend Tribune**. I was flattered that Mary was always so enthusiastic whenever I turned in a column. Bill and Nancy Nich of the **Mishawaka Enterprise** also eagerly published several of these essays.

I have many thanks to extend also to my parents, Joe and Mary Ann De Kever, who have patiently endured and encouraged my various historical quests and crusades over the years. They brought me to the first historical event I was present at: Robert F. Kennedy's rally in downtown Mishawaka. My mother was eight months pregnant with me, so I could not see or hear very well, but I am proud to say I was there. My father filmed the Spell Bowl and social studies competitions, which helped in reconstructing the sequence of events in those rounds. They also offered editorial advice regarding these essays when they were originally written and when they were revised in the summer of 2002.

I am grateful to the dozens of people who gave their time and insight to help compete these essays. While they should feel a strong sense of ownership in this finished product, I alone am responsible for any errors of accuracy or omission.

PHOTO CREDITS

136: author
142: Mishawaka-Penn-Harris
     Public Library
144: author
145: author
148: Mishawaka-Penn-Harris
     Public Library
149: Mishawaka-Penn-Harris
     Public Library
151: Mishawaka-Penn-Harris
     Public Library
154: Mishawaka-Penn-Harris
     Public Library
166: author
168: Grace Hill
170: Jim Lang
171: Jim Lang
173: Grace Hill

176: author
177: author
181: Mishawaka-Penn-Harris
     Public Library
190: author
191: author
192: author
198: author
201: author
206: author
207: author
211: author
222: author
223: author
224: author
232: author
234: author
237: author